MW00471548

Christian History Made Easy

Leader Guide

Timothy Paul Jones, PhD

Developed with Jennifer R. Garrison

This Leader Guide accompanies the

Christian History Made Easy 12-session DVD-based study
(ISBN 9781596365254 or ISBN 9781596365261)

and

Christian History Made Easy Participant Guide
(ISBN 9781596365285)

March 2015

ROSE
PUBLISHING

© 2012 Bristol Works, Inc.

Rose Publishing, Inc.

4733 Torrance Blvd., #259

Torrance, California 90503 U.S.A.

Email: info@rose-publishing.com

www.rose-publishing.com

Register your Rose Publishing books at

www.rose-publishing.com/register.

Scripture taken from the New American Standard Bible, ©Copyright 1960, 1962, 1963, 1968, 1971, 1972, 1973, 1975, 1977, 1995 by the Lockman Foundation. Used by permission.

Author Timothy Paul Jones is represented by Nappaland Literary Agency www.nappaland.com.

Printed in the United States of America

Contents

About This Study

"We have," the author of Hebrews remarked, "so great a cloud of witnesses surrounding us" (Heb. 12:1). The Apostles' Creed echoes, "I believe ... in the communion of the saints."

What these ancient words seem to suggest is that when Christians gather, it isn't only the living that are present. In some way that transcends human understanding, the saints of the past are present too. Their presence around us points us toward Jesus Christ, "the author and perfecter of our faith" (Heb. 12:2). This cloud has grown far fuller since the first century AD, as millions who have embraced the gospel have faced death and found themselves "at home with the Lord" (2 Cor. 5:8). Together, these many men and women form the history of Christianity—a vast and beautiful story that is, if you are a Christian, your story too!

Yet many Christians find it difficult to make sense of this story. The history of Christianity can seem overwhelming, confusing, even boring—but, in truth, this story is far from boring! The history of Christianity is the story of reformers and revivalists, martyrs and crusaders. It's the true story of how the good news of Jesus has spread around the globe. It's the story of God's Spirit working through ordinary people in extraordinary ways. This story enables God's people to read their Bibles better, to evaluate their beliefs more wisely, and to understand why other Christians do what they do. The purpose of this study is to introduce you to this exciting story in a way that anyone can understand and enjoy.

This study is designed for twelve 60-minute sessions with the video portion for each session lasting 25–35 minutes. The teaching time can be expanded to twelve 90-minute sessions by using the *Christian History Made Easy* PowerPoint® presentation or other study materials included in the *Christian History Made Easy* Complete Kit. (At the end of this Leader Guide there are suggestions for leading an additional session for groups that plan on meeting for thirteen weeks.)

Participant Guides for class members contain: session outlines to follow along with the video, key terms and definitions, charts, study questions and activities for further learning.

About the Author

Dr. Timothy Paul Jones

Timothy Paul Jones is a bestselling and award-winning author, scholar, and professor of leadership at The Southern Baptist Theological Seminary. He has earned the Bachelor of Arts degree in biblical studies and pastoral ministry, the Master of Divinity with focus in history and New Testament, as well as the Doctor of Philosophy.

Dr. Jones has authored, coauthored, or contributed to more than a dozen books. He has also written numerous articles for popular ministry magazines and academic journals including *Discipleship Journal, Religious Education Journal, Christian Education Journal,* and *Perspectives in Religious Studies.* Dr. Jones has contributed to two highly-regarded reference works, *Nelson's Dictionary of Christianity* and *Nelson's New Christian Dictionary.* He has been the recipient of the Baker Book House Award, the North American Professors of Christian Education Scholastic Recognition Award, and the 2009 Retailers' Choice Award from *Christian Retailing* magazine.

Despite his strong academic pedigree, Dr. Jones has shown a unique ability to communicate in an appealing, accessible style through books such as the award-winning *Christian History Made Easy* and the best selling *The Da Vinci Codebreaker* (coauthored with James Garlow). Dr. Jones has been featured on Fox News and WGN, commenting on religious trends and topics. He is represented by Nappaland Literary Agency (www.nappaland.com) and blogs at www.timothypauljones.com.

Dr. Jones resides in Louisville, Kentucky, with his wife Rayann and daughters Hannah and Skylar. Over the past two decades, he has had the privilege of serving as a pastor in several churches. In these contexts, he saw how learning about theology and church history could help Christians to flesh out their faith in amazing ways.

Leader Guide developed with Jennifer R. Garrison

Jennifer R. Garrison is adjunct instructor in the School of Theology at Campbellsville University. She has earned two master's degrees from Southwestern Baptist Theological Seminary, one in Christian Education and the other in Ministry-Based Evangelism. She is also a candidate for the Doctor of Philosophy at The Southern Baptist Theological Seminary. Jennifer resides in Campbellsville, Kentucky, with her husband Shane and their two sons, Isaac and Ethan.

Get the Complete DVD-Based Kit

The Kit (ISBN 9781596365254) includes everything you need to teach *Christian History Made Easy* using professionally produced video sessions, leader and participant guides, and a PowerPoint® presentation.

The Kit includes:

- DVD with 12 video sessions

- One printed *Christian History Made Easy* participant guide (ISBN 9781596365285)

- One printed *Christian History Made Easy* leader guide (ISBN 9781596365278) + PDF leader guide

- One printed copy of the award-winning, full-color *Christian History Made Easy* handbook (ISBN 9781596363281)

- *Christian History Made Easy* PowerPoint® presentation on CD-ROM (ISBN 9781596363410)

- PDF files for posters, fliers, handouts, and bulletin inserts for promotion

Available at www.ChristianHistoryMadeEasy.com or www.rose-publishing.com or by calling Rose Publishing at 1-800-532-4278. Also available wherever good Christian books are sold.

Register your Rose Publishing books at www.rose-publishing.com/register.

Session 1
The First Christians
AD 1–100

Why on earth does history matter, anyway? History matters because it's the story of how God works among his people in his world!

In the first century AD, two specific historical events—a fire in Rome and the fall of Jerusalem—caused Christians to be seen as a separate and dangerous sect. Roman governors and emperors mocked Christians, threw them to the beasts, and burned them at the stake. Yet, no matter what anyone did, God remained present among his people, working at every turn to cause the gospel to spread through the testimony of the church.

Session 1 Outline

1. History matters because:

    a. The gospel matters. The gospel is rooted in historical events.

    b. God's Word matters. The better we understand history, the better we can apply God's Word.

    c. God's work matters. History reminds us that God's work includes more than our own generation.

2. What happened after Acts 28?

    a. Persecution after the fire in Rome, AD 64 (Nero)

    b. Division after the fall of Jerusalem, AD 70 (Vespasian, Titus)

    c. Deification of emperors in their lifetimes, AD 81–96 (Domitian)

    d. Deepening persecution of Christians; Ignatius, Polycarp, and Blandina martyred.

Roman Emperors

Emperor	Reign	Description	Death
Nero	AD 54–68	The first part of his reign was peaceful, but in the second part he ordered the deaths of his chief advisors, many wealthy nobles, and even his own mother. When a massive fire in Rome struck in AD 64, he avoided culpability by blaming the Christians for it and ruthlessly persecuting them. Paul and Peter are believed to have been martyred during Nero's persecution.	Committed suicide
Vespasian	AD 69–79	Ruler after Nero who was instrumental in quelling a Jewish uprising in Jerusalem and eventually ordering his son Titus to destroy Jerusalem and the temple.	Died of illness
Titus	AD 79–81	One of Vespasian's sons, who as a military leader before becoming emperor, destroyed the temple in Jerusalem in AD 70.	Died of illness
Domitian	AD 81–96	Vespasian's youngest son, he is known for being the first emperor to demand the title "lord and god" of himself. (Traditionally, emperors were deified after their death.) He severely persecuted Christians in the later part of his reign.	Assassinated

Before the Gathering

- Obtain a *Christian History Made Easy* Participant Guide (ISBN 9781596365285) for each class member.

- In the *Christian History Made Easy* handbook, read the Introduction "Why Does Church History Matter?" and chapter 1.

- Preview the video segment Session 1 and PowerPoint® presentation chapter 1.

- Study Hebrews 11:1–12:2 and Revelation 22:13. Incorporate in your notes and discussion a few facts that you learned from this study.

- Complete the lesson in the Participant Guide for this session.

- If you will be using the video or PowerPoint® presentation, ensure that components are connected and tested beforehand.

- Pray for guidance as you lead this session.

Goals for the Gathering

Through this session, participants will be able to:

- Articulate the importance of learning about great individuals and historical movements that have brought Christians to their present place in history.

- Gain a new understanding of the "great cloud of witnesses" as this "cloud" continues to grow to include all who follow Jesus Christ.

- Examine their own lives and consider their role in the present church and how they will one day be identified among "the great cloud of witnesses."

Get Them Talking   (10 minutes)

Read Hebrews 11:1–12:2 and Revelation 22:13. Since the passage from Hebrews is lengthy, consider creative ways of looking at this text together, such as (1) organize your group into smaller groups of two or three and have each group read a small section of the passage; each group can then summarize for the whole group; (2) print the passage and read it aloud—responsively or in unison—as a group. Focus attention on Hebrews 12:1–2.

Take a Closer Look   (30 to 60 minutes)

Watch the video segment for Session 1. (30 minutes)

Optional: Review the content of the video using the PowerPoint® presentation chapter 1. (30 minutes)

Seek the Central Truth   (15 minutes)

The "great cloud of witnesses"! Who can be found in this number? After those included in the list of witnesses found in Hebrews 11, many other Christ-followers have been added. According to one tradition, Simon Peter felt unworthy of the honor of a death identical to that of Christ, and said, "I beg you executioners, crucify me thus, with the head downward and not otherwise." His famous request to be crucified upside down was heard and represents an example of true humility and great love for his Savior.

Paul likewise died for the sake of Christ. Though his Roman citizenship likely kept him from death by crucifixion, he was martyred nonetheless. Paul, like Peter and many who have come after him, gave his life so the gospel could go forward. Their refusal to renounce Christ resulted in their death, but God used their faithfulness to expand the reach of the gospel.

Consider the following statements from history about Peter and Paul: "Peter, because of others' unrighteous envy, endured not one or two, but numerous labors; and when he had at length suffered martyrdom, departed to the place of glory due to him.... Paul also obtained the reward of patient endurance, after being seven times thrown into captivity, compelled to flee, and stoned. After preaching both in the east and west, he gained the illustrious reputation due to his faith, having taught righteousness to the whole world, and come to the extreme limit of the west, and suffered martyrdom under the prefects" (Clement, *To the Corinthians*, 5).

Peter and Paul are only two examples of Christ-followers who now stand among the "great cloud of witnesses." Their great love for Christ drove them to great sacrifice. And great as their sacrifices were, they were still incomparable to the greatest sacrifice of all, given by Jesus Christ.

Wrap It Up   (5 minutes)

End your time together with a prayer similar to this one: "God, we thank you for the men and women of history who make up the great cloud of witnesses. Thank you for leaving to us a record of their example. Help us to examine our own lives and to respond faithfully to the goodness you have shown us in Jesus Christ. Work in us to press the gospel forward in our everyday lives, as so many have done who have come before us. In the name of Jesus Christ our Lord, Amen."

Strongly encourage class members to complete the Participant Guide activities for this week (Session 1).

Optional: Obtain a prayer update from ministries that serve persecuted Christians, for example, Voice of the Martyrs www.persecution.com or Open Doors www.opendoorsusa.org. Remind participants that Christianity is not Western, Eastern, or American—it's a global faith. Praying for persecuted Christians is one of the most powerful things we can do for our brothers and sisters around the world—and it's the number one thing persecuted believers ask for! Pray together as a group or, if time is short, ask participants to commit to praying at least once in the coming week for a specific region or country where Christians face persecution.

Work Together

Sacrificial living and giving is a common thread that runs throughout Scripture and church history. Sacrifice your time and energy this week by serving as a group in your church or community to honor those who have gone on before. Take time to walk through your church or community cemetery, cleaning and straightening as needed. Select one or more graves of individuals with living relatives that are still part of your church or community to decorate with flowers or plants. Discuss the spiritual heritage that the individual has left to your community. Reach out to the individual's living relatives, and communicate to them how that person has impacted you, your church, or your community.

SESSION 2
Defending the Truth
AD *100–300*

Roman persecutions dogged God's people from the outside! False teachings hounded the church from within! Faced with such challenging circumstances, Christians faced several crucial questions: Which writings should be seen as authoritative? Was Jesus really fully God and fully man? What does it mean to be a Christian?

These were not heady debates, limited to a few Bible colleges and theological seminaries. These were deeply practical struggles in local churches to maintain the truth of Jesus at a time when proclaiming the gospel could cost Christians their lives.

Session 2 Outline

1. Orthodoxy and Heresy

   a. Walter Bauer's hypothesis

2. Four False Perspectives on Jesus

   a. Ebionites ("poor ones")

   b. Docetists ("I seem")

   c. Gnostics ("in the know")

   d. Marcionism

3. Three Ways that Christians Responded

   a. Canon of Scripture

      i. Can the text be traced to an eyewitness or a close associate of an eyewitness?
      ii. Do other congregations accept this text as a testimony that can be traced to an eyewitness or a close associate of an eyewitness?
      iii. Does this text agree with other texts that can be traced without any doubt to an eyewitness or a close associate of an eyewitness?

   b. Confession of Faith

      i. A series of questions asked at baptism that later developed into the Apostles' Creed.

   c. Centralized Authority

      i. Overseers (bishops) oversaw multiple congregations and traced their teachings back to the apostles.

Key Terms

Apostles' Creed – Early Christian confession of faith. This confession was not written by the apostles. The name "Apostles' Creed" means that the creed contains the truths that the apostles taught. Though the date the creed was written remains unknown, similar statements in the creed can be found in the second-century AD "Rule of Faith."

Bishop – Church leader responsible for looking after a church's faithfulness. Interchangeable with "elder" or "pastor" among early Christians (Acts 20:17–28; 1 Peter 5:1–3).

Canon – (*kanon*, "measuring stick") Group of writings that God inspired to tell the story of Jesus and to mark out the boundaries of Christian beliefs.

Docetism – (*dokeo*, "to seem") Heresy that claimed that Jesus only seemed to possess a physical body.

Ebionism – (*ebyonim*, "poor ones") Heresy that claimed that Jesus was a human Messiah, but not divine, and that God adopted Jesus at his baptism.

Gnosticism – (*gnostikos*, "knowing") Heresy that claimed that the creator of the physical world was evil, and only secret knowledge can reconnect people with the supreme deity.

"Gospel of Peter" – An early second century AD writing that was rejected as an authoritative account of Jesus' life because it could not be clearly connected to the apostle Peter and because some passages in the book could be misconstrued to suggest that Jesus wasn't fully human. Perhaps partially preserved in Codex Papyrus Cairo 10759.

Gospel – (*godspel*, "good message") The life, death, and resurrection of Jesus by which God establishes his kingdom in the world and makes sinners right with himself through faith.

Heresy – (*hairesis*, "choosing a sect") A teaching that contradicts the essential truths about Jesus as believed and proclaimed by the apostles.

Inerrancy – Belief that the inspired human authors of the Scriptures never affirmed anything contrary to fact when writing the texts that became part of the biblical canon. As a result, Christians can be confident that the Bible never errs.

Marcionism – (from Marcion of Sinope, an early leader) Heresy that claimed that the God of the Old Testament and the God of the New Testament were two different deities.

Muratorian Fragment — Possibly the oldest list of the books included in the New Testament canon, dating to the mid-second century AD. It lists all four Gospels, Acts, and Paul's 13 epistles.

Orthodox — (*orthos* [straight] + *doxa* [opinion, expectation]) The essential truths about Jesus that were proclaimed by the apostles and preserved by early Christians.

Shepherd of Hermas — Popular second-century AD Christian writing. Some Christians thought it should be read alongside the books that would later be recognized as the New Testament. The Muratorian Fragment reveals why this text was not recognized as an authoritative text for Christians: "Hermas composed Shepherd quite recently—in our own times, in the city of Rome.... So while it should indeed be read, it ought not to be read publicly for the people of the church—it is counted neither among the [Old Testament] prophets (for their number has been completed) nor among the apostles (for it is after their time)."

Before the Gathering

- In the *Christian History Made Easy* handbook, read chapter 2.

- Preview the video segment Session 2 and the PowerPoint® presentation chapter 2.

- Study Galatians 1:1–12. Incorporate in your notes and discussion a few facts that you learned from this study.

- Complete the lesson in the Participant Guide for this session.

- If you will be using the video or PowerPoint® presentation, ensure that components are connected and tested beforehand.

- Locate the article "A Call for Theological Triage and Christian Maturity" at www.albertmohler.com. Print a copy of the article for each participant.

- Pray for guidance as you lead this session.

Goals for the Gathering

Through this session, participants will be able to:

- Articulate to a skeptic how the canon of Scripture was formed.

- Describe the process by which eyewitness testimony about Jesus was preserved among the early churches.

- Acknowledge that Scripture is a unique and authoritative testimony that provides perfect and unerring testimony to God's work in history, particularly God's work in and through Jesus Christ.

Get Them Talking (10 minutes)

Read Galatians 1:1–12. Consider the following questions to kick off your discussion:

- What benefit do readers of the New Testament today have that the first readers of the New Testament did not have? [Guide the class toward recognizing the wonderful gift of God's written Word, completed and freely available in a single volume.]

- Paul identifies himself in a similar way in both verses 1 and 12. Why was it so important for Paul to identify himself in this way? [Help students to see the importance of eyewitness testimony about Jesus among early Christians.]

- Paul confronts the Galatians because they have turned from the true gospel to a false gospel, which was really no gospel at all. If Paul could directly confront Christians today, what might he say about the gospel in our churches?

- In what ways should the contemporary church contend for biblical truth?

Take a Closer Look (30 to 60 minutes)

Watch the video segment for Session 2. (35 minutes)

Optional: Review the content of the video using the PowerPoint® presentation chapter 2. (25 minutes)

Seek the Central Truth (15 minutes)

At the time of Paul's writing, the Christian faith was in its infancy. Even though the gospel was first revealed in the book of Genesis (3:15), the clear gospel message of salvation through explicit faith in Jesus Christ seemed new. Some groups claimed to be Christ-followers but they attempted to alter the message that could be traced back to eyewitnesses. For centuries, the followers of Jesus found themselves constantly defending the gospel first proclaimed by Jesus and his apostles. Does any part of this scenario sound familiar? This ancient battle is also a contemporary battle! The church of today must still stand firmly in defense of the Truth.

In the middle of the first century AD, a mere two decades after Jesus called his first apostles, Paul made a clear case that followers of Jesus in Galatia must reject any so-called gospel that could not be traced back to authoritative eyewitnesses of the risen Lord Jesus. Paul even declared that anyone who altered the gospel would be cursed by God! The gospel that is proclaimed through our lives today and through the church must be the same good news that Paul proclaimed to the Galatians. It must be God's truth graciously demonstrated to humanity through the life, death, and resurrection of Jesus Christ, nothing more and nothing less.

Together: Work through the article "A Call for Theological Triage and Christian Maturity." Discuss several issues that churches face. Determine in which of the three categories each issue belongs:

1. First-level issues are gospel issues, to deny any of these truths is to deny the faith or to place oneself so directly at odds with Scripture that the integrity of the gospel is at stake. (Examples: humanity of Jesus, deity of Jesus, salvation by grace through faith)

2. Second-level issues are issues where faithful Christians disagree, but the disagreements deeply affect how these Christians practice their faith in their churches. It's unlikely that Christians will be able to serve together in the same church if they disagree about second-level issues. (Examples: whether infants are baptized, whether women are ordained as pastors, whether supernatural spiritual gifts ended in the first-century AD or if they continue still today)

3. Third-level issues are issues where Christians even in the same local church should agree to disagree peaceably. (Examples: musical styles in worship, specific views on the end times, whether the earth is few thousand years old or a few billion)

Wrap It Up   (5 minutes)

End your time together with a prayer similar to this one: "We give thanks to you, our Lord and our God, for revealing Jesus to us through your Word. We praise you for the ways that you have used ordinary people for the extraordinary purpose of preserving your truth. Work in us through your Word and through your Spirit. Reveal yourself in our lives. Convict us by your Spirit when we fail to see the sufficiency of the gospel. Work in us to trust you more. In the name of Jesus Christ our Lord, Amen."

Strongly encourage students to complete the Participant Guide activities for this week.

Optional: Pray together as a group for persecuted Christians or, if time is short, ask participants to commit to praying at least once in the coming week for a specific region or country where our brothers and sisters face persecution.

Work Together

How blessed we are to hold a copy of God's Word in our hands! The earliest Christians probably could not have imagined carrying a single volume that contained the words of the apostolic eyewitnesses about Jesus. Most church members today own multiple copies of the Bible, yet some families in your community may not even possess one copy of the Bible that they can easily read.

Consider serving your community this week by sharing Bibles with those in need. If possible, gather new Bibles. If that's not possible for your group, compile unused copies from your own personal collections. Determine how you will distribute the Bibles, perhaps focusing on one particular neighborhood or choosing specific un-churched homes. Once the Bibles are distributed, earnestly pray for those who received them. Consider a follow-up visit with the families. Offer to share your favorite Scripture passages, to answer questions they have regarding what they have read, or to show them how to find particular verses or passages in the Bible.

Session 3
Persecuted to Preferred

AD *300–500*

After decades of experiencing vicious persecution, Christianity suddenly became the preferred religion of the Roman Empire! The story goes that Emperor Constantine saw a vision in the sky, chalked a Christian symbol on his soldiers' shields, then began crediting the God of the Christians for his military victories. Constantine actively promoted Christianity and even convened the first church-wide council in which Christian leaders from across the empire met at Nicaea to deal with heresies—but these changes came at a cost. When it came to maintaining the purity of the gospel, imperial favor wasn't always as favorable as it had seemed at first.

Session 3 Outline

1. How Roman Persecution of Christians Ended

    a. Emperor Diocletian planned for peace by splitting the empire into East and West (AD 286).

    b. On his deathbed, Emperor Galerius decreed that the persecution of Christians should end (AD 311).

    c. Constantine conquered Rome with a Christian symbol on his soldiers' shields (AD 312) and his Edict of Milan legalized Christianity (AD 313).

2. The Problem with Arius

    a. Arius taught that Jesus was a lesser being than God the Father.

    b. Council of Nicaea rejected Arius' teachings (AD 325).

    c. Athanasius stood up to Emperor Constantine when Constantine wanted to allow Arius back in the church.

Key Terms

Arianism – (from Arius, founder of the movement) Heretical belief that Jesus was created and that his divinity was not equal to God the Father.

Chi-Rho – (Latin *chiron*) In the fourth century, Emperor Constantine popularized the Chi-Rho symbol. It is a Christian symbol made from two Greek letters, Chi (X) and Rho (P), which are the first two letters of "Christ" in Greek (ΧΡΙΣΤΟΣ or *Christos*). These two letters were also the first two letters of a common name that meant "useful" (ΧΡΗΣΤΟΣ or *Chrestos*). Constantine may have used the Chi-Rho because it had a double meaning that Christians saw as an expression of their faith, while others would simply see it as a reference to strength or usefulness.

Council of Nicaea (AD 325) – First ecumenical (church-wide) council; called by Emperor Constantine in the city of Nicaea (in modern-day Turkey) to deal with the teachings of an elder named Arius. The council overwhelmingly denounced Arianism and formulated the Creed of Nicaea.

Edict of Milan (AD 313) – Letter signed by emperors Constantine and Licinius that legalized all religions in the Roman Empire, including Christianity. This effectively ended Christian persecution by emperors.

Heresy – (from *hairesis*, "choosing a sect") A teaching that contradicts the essential truths about Jesus as believed and proclaimed by the apostles.

Monk – (from *monakhos*, "alone") In the fourth century, a man who isolated himself in the deserts to diminish temptations and to become closer to God.

Orthodox – (*orthos* [straight] + *doxa* [opinion, expectation]) The essential truths about Jesus that were proclaimed by the apostles and preserved by early Christians.

Trinity – Christian doctrine that teaches there is one God who exists eternally in three Persons: God the Father, God the Son, and God the Holy Spirit.

Before the Gathering

- In the *Christian History Made Easy* handbook, read chapter 3.

- Preview the video segment Session 3 and PowerPoint® presentation chapter 3.

- Study Matthew 28:19, 1 Corinthians 12:4–6, 2 Corinthians 13:14, and Ephesians 4:4–6. Incorporate into your notes and discussion a few facts that you learned from this study.

- Complete the lesson in the Participant Guide for this session.

- If you will be using the video or PowerPoint® presentation, ensure that components are connected and tested beforehand.

- Locate the article "Sorry, Athanasius, It's Not Over" at www.albertmohler. com and "Carson and Keller on Jakes and the Elephant Room" at www. thegospelcoalition.org. Print a copy of articles for each participant. Become familiar with the controversies described in these articles so that you can provide participants with background information. Use these articles to demonstrate how false teachers within the church attempt to dilute or even to deny doctrines such as the Trinity or the deity of Jesus even today.

- Pray for guidance as you lead this session.

Goals for the Gathering

Through this session, participants will be able to:

- Understand the significant historical measures taken by the early church leaders to declare and preserve biblical truth.

- Appreciate the importance of a fundamental truth of the Christian faith, that God is one God eternally existing in three persons.

- Identify areas in their own lives that are impacted when people downplay biblical truth.

Get Them Talking   (10 minutes)

Read Matthew 28:19, 1 Corinthians 12:4–6, 2 Corinthians 13:14, and Ephesians 4:4–6. None of these passages uses the term "Trinity," but all of them imply this fundamental truth.

Consider the following questions for discussion starters:

- Why does the doctrine of the Trinity matter to your personal faith in Christ?

- Has there ever been a time when you have met someone who has questioned the doctrine of the Trinity?

- Historically, some have claimed that Jesus was not of the same essence (or, substance) as the God the Father. This would mean that the deity of Jesus is lower or lesser than the deity of God the Father. How does this claim differ from the teaching of Scripture?

- Provide some examples of clear biblical truths that are diluted or denied today.

Take a Closer Look   (30 to 60 minutes)

Watch the video segment Session 3. (30 minutes)

Optional: Review the content of the video using the PowerPoint® presentation chapter 3. (30 minutes)

Seek the Central Truth   (15 minutes)

You and I live in an era in which the culture expects people to be "tolerant," but this cultural tolerance doesn't mean simply living peaceably and lovingly alongside people with whom you disagree. What is demanded by the new tolerance is that we express acceptance and approval of beliefs and lifestyles that we don't agree with. One of the most offensive claims that a person can make today is to assert that absolute truth does exist and that this truth is found in Jesus Christ, as he has been revealed to us through the Scriptures.

During the early fourth century AD, Christianity became legal, and the number of people in churches multiplied. Disagreements multiplied as well. One such disagreement had to do with the Trinity. Some church members claimed that Jesus Christ and God the Father were not equally eternal or equally divine. In one sense, this matter had been settled in the first century, because the New Testament writings clearly taught that Jesus was fully human yet fully divine. The Council of Nicaea in AD 325 reaffirmed this ancient teaching and issued a confession of faith to express these truths in a memorable way.

Together: Look at the articles that you located and printed earlier. Provide participants with background information that they may need to understand the articles. Use these articles as foundations for discussing how false teachers within the church attempt to dilute or even to deny doctrines such as the Trinity or the deity of Jesus even today.

Wrap It Up (5 minutes)

End your time together with a prayer similar to this one: "God, we praise you for raising up leaders in the past who, in spite of their weaknesses, pointed your people to your truth. Never let us forget that it is only through your grace that we can stand strong in your truth. Make us wise, make us loving, make us bold, so that we may stand without apology for your Word and for the gospel. In the name of Jesus Christ our Lord, Amen."

Strongly encourage class members to complete the Participant Guide activities for this week.

Optional: Pray together as a group for persecuted Christians or, if time is short, ask participants to commit to praying at least once in the coming week for a specific region or country where our brothers and sisters face persecution. (See suggestion below)

Work Together

Many places in the world enjoy widespread religious freedom. Other regions, however, are hotbeds of persecution. Christians are ostracized by their families, tortured, and even murdered for their faith in Christ. Prayerfully select an area of the world where Christians are persecuted. Organize a three-to-six hour prayer event, divided into half-hour time slots. Encourage each group member to fill one time slot. The group members will spend the assigned time praying over specific needs that you have researched beforehand and developed into a prayer guide.

SESSION 4
Christianity on the Move
AD *300–500*

It's one thing to live as a Christian in a world where your faith is persecuted and oppressed. Life may be hard but the boundaries between belief and unbelief are fairly clear. It's quite another to be faithful when the name "Christian" is not persecuted but praised, and even endowed with power!

Some Christians responded to this new state of affairs by moving to monastic communities deep in the deserts of Egypt and North Africa. Meanwhile, barbarians from Asia and northern Europe were migrating southward into the Western Empire. As Rome was repeatedly sacked and the Western Empire fragmented, Christian leaders like Augustine helped believers to take a new perspective on the powers that surrounded them.

Session 4 Outline

1. Monks Moved to the Desert.

    a. Gregory of Nazianzus joined Basil's monastic community.

    b. Apollinaris taught that Jesus did not have a human spirit; Gregory of Nazianzus argued against this heresy.

    c. Council of Constantinople (AD 381): Jesus was recognized once again as fully God and fully man.

2. Roman Empire Fell to Barbarians.

    a. Barbarians moved south and west into the Roman Empire.

    b. Visigoth barbarians sacked Rome (AD 410).

    c. Augustine of Hippo wrote *The City of God* to help Christians respond to the charge that Christianity caused the fall of Rome.

3. Church Councils and Controversies Continued.

    a. Council of Ephesus (AD 431): Jesus was one person.

    b. Council of Chalcedon (AD 451): Jesus had two natures.

4. Monks and Nuns Preserved Learning.

    a. Benedict and Scholastica established monasteries that included schools.

    b. Gregory became the first bishop of Rome from a monastic background and one of the first individuals to exercise the power that would become associated with the title "pope" (AD 590).

Key Terms

Apollinarianism – (from Apollinaris, early proponent) Heretical belief that Jesus possessed a human body, but the divine Word replaced his human mind, so that Jesus did not have a human spirit. Form of monophysitism.

Benedictine Rule – Developed by Benedict of Nursia, it provided precepts for monastic communities that included, not primarily solitude, but rhythms of rest, work, and study of Scripture. It shaped monasticism in the Middle Ages.

Catholic – (from Greek, *kath'olou*, "according to the whole") Worldwide, accepted by all; originally a reference to the beliefs and patterns embraced by all Christians throughout the world.

Dyophysitism – (from Greek, "two natures") Orthodox belief that Jesus has two natures, one human and one divine, which work in perfect harmony with one another.

Eutychianism – (after Eutyches, early proponent) Heretical belief that Jesus' divine nature absorbed his human nature to form one mixed nature. Form of monophysitism.

Great Cappadocians – Eastern Church leaders who helped fourth-century Christians clarify their beliefs about the Trinity.

Monk – (from *monakhos*, "alone") At first, a man who isolated himself in the deserts to diminish temptations and to become closer to God.

Monophysitism – (from Greek, "one nature") Heretical belief that Jesus had only one nature instead of having both a human nature and a divine nature.

Nestorianism – (after Nestorius, accused of teaching this view) Heretical belief that Jesus was two persons in one body. More properly known as hyper-dyophysitism. A popular title for the Virgin Mary was *Theotokos* meaning "bearer of God." Nestorius however preferred *Christokos* meaning "bearer of the Messiah." This controversy eventually lead to the Council of Ephesus.

Nun – (from *nonna*, Latin for an elderly tutor) A woman who joined a religious community, vowing obedience and choosing not to marry or to own property.

Pope – (from Latin for "father") At first, title for any bishop in a major city. As the Roman church's power grew in the Western Empire, it became the title for the bishop of Rome.

The Vulgate – The Latin version of the Bible translated by Jerome in the fourth century AD. It became the most commonly used translation of the Bible in the Roman Catholic Church in the Middle Ages.

Church Councils in the Fourth and Fifth Centuries

Council	Year	Issue	Conclusion
Nicaea	325	Arianism	First church-wide council, produced the Creed of Nicaea; Jesus is equal to God the Father.
Constantinople	381	Apollinarianism	Second church-wide council, approved the Nicene Creed; Jesus was both human and divine.
Ephesus	431	Nestorianism	Third church-wide council, clarified that Jesus was one person not two persons in one body.
Chalcedon	451	Eutychianism	Fourth church-wide council, clarified that, though Jesus was one person, he possessed human and divine natures.

Before the Gathering

- In the *Christian History Made Easy* handbook, read chapter 4.

- Preview the video segment Session 4 and PowerPoint® presentation chapter 4.

- Study John 1:14, Hebrews 1:2–3 and 4:15, Colossians 1:15–20, Luke 2:52, Matthew 4:2, John 19:28, and John 11:33–35. Summarize what each passage teaches about the deity or the humanity of Jesus. Incorporate in your notes and discussion a few facts that you learned from this study.

- Complete the lesson in the Participant Guide for this session.

- If you will be using the video or PowerPoint® presentation, ensure that components are connected and tested beforehand.

- Print or photocopy the Nicene Creed for each participant (see p. 34; also in Participant Guide).

- Pray for guidance as you lead this session.

Goals for the Gathering

Through this session, participants will be able to:

- Describe how God spread the gospel through the lives of monks and nuns.

- Explain how God used specific leaders in the church to clarify the truth about who Jesus is.

- Consider how God is working specifically in their own lives to grow his kingdom.

Get Them Talking (10 minutes)

Organize the following passages among two or more groups: John 1:14, Hebrews 1:2–3 and 4:15, Colossians 1:15–20, Luke 2:52, Matthew 4:2, John 19:28, and John 11:33–35. Have each group decide which of their assigned texts identify *Jesus as fully God* and which emphasize *Jesus as fully human*. Help the groups to see how Scripture, when taken as a whole, affirms that Jesus was one person but that he had two natures, one human and one divine.

Consider the following discussion starters:

- What are some core beliefs that Christians should accept about who Jesus is?

- List every Christian creed or confession of faith that you can recall. What role do creeds and confessions of faith play in your church?

Take a Closer Look (30 to 60 minutes)

Watch the video segment Session 4. (35 minutes)

Optional: Review the content of the video using the PowerPoint® presentation chapter 4. (25 minutes)

Seek the Central Truth (15 minutes)

Even in the early centuries of Christianity, some people didn't understand who Jesus was; still today, many people are unclear. Jehovah's Witnesses hold an Arian view of Jesus. Mormons see Jesus in ways that are similar to Arianism and some ancient forms of Gnosticism. Some churches that use many of the same terminologies as orthodox believers actually have a modalist or oneness view of God, which means that they deny essential distinctions between God the Father, God the Son, and God the Holy Spirit.

Here's what orthodox Christians throughout the ages have believed about Jesus:

- Jesus is one person who exists eternally and equally with the persons of God the Father and God the Holy Spirit. They are one God.

- Jesus has two natures: one human and one divine.

- Jesus is fully God.

- Jesus is fully human.

Views of Jesus in Christian History

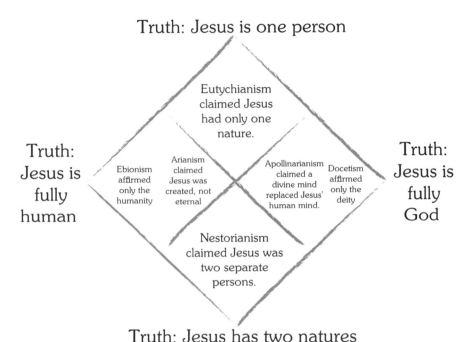

Truth: Jesus is one person

Eutychianism claimed Jesus had only one nature.

Truth: Jesus is fully human

Ebionism affirmed only the humanity

Arianism claimed Jesus was created, not eternal

Apollinarianism claimed a divine mind replaced Jesus' human mind.

Docetism affirmed only the deity

Truth: Jesus is fully God

Nestorianism claimed Jesus was two separate persons.

Truth: Jesus has two natures

Carefully examine the chart above. Discuss together why each of the four truths about Jesus (one person, two natures, fully human, fully divine) is still important for Christians today. (Chart also in Participant Guide)

Organize into three groups. Instruct each group to look at one of the three sections of the Nicene Creed. Have each group write a prayer to the Lord, praising him for the traits mentioned in their assigned section of the Nicene Creed. For example, "We praise you Lord because you are _____."

Wrap It Up (5 minutes)

End your time together by praising God, using the three prayers that the groups wrote based on the Nicene Creed.

Strongly encourage class members to complete the Participant Guide activities for this week.

Optional: Pray together as a group for persecuted Christians or, if time is short, ask participants to commit to praying at least once in the coming week for a specific region or country where our brothers and sisters face persecution.

Work Together

For centuries followers of Christ have committed themselves to the ministry of sharing God's Word. This week, serve your community in a similar manner. Choose two or three individuals from your community who are committed to Christ but who, because of some impairment, cannot read the Bible themselves. Visit them and read passages from Scripture to them.

The Nicene Creed

The "Symbol of the Faith" from the Council of Constantinople (AD 381), based on the Creed of Nicaea (AD 325)

"We believe in one God,
the Father Almighty,
Maker of heaven and earth,
and of all things visible and invisible."

"We believe in one Lord,
Jesus Christ the One and Only Son of God,
begotten of the Father before all ages,
light of light, very God of very God,
begotten not created,
being of the same essence with the Father;
by him all things were made;
he for us men and for our salvation came down;
he was incarnate by the Holy Spirit of the Virgin Mary;
he was made man;
he was crucified for us under Pontius Pilate;
he suffered death and was buried;
the third day he rose again according to the Scriptures,
ascended into heaven, and sits at the Father's right hand;
from there, he will return in glory to judge the living and the dead;
his kingdom will have no end."

"We believe in the Holy Spirit,
the Lord and Giver of life,
who proceeds from the Father,
who together with the Father and the Son is worshiped and glorified,
who spoke by the prophets, and in one, holy, catholic, apostolic Church;
we acknowledge one baptism unto remission of sins;
we look for the resurrection of the dead
and the life of the world to come."

SESSION 5
A Church Divided

AD *500–1300*

The East and West grew further apart! King and bishops grew more deeply entwined! Kings forced professions of faith, and popes called for brutal Crusades! But these Crusades, far from unifying East and West, climaxed with the shattering of Christianity into two communions, Eastern Orthodox and Roman Catholic.

Session 5 Outline

1. Icon Controversy

2. The Franks

    a. Charlemagne (Charles the Great) forced Christian conversions.

    b. Pope Leo III crowned Charlemagne as emperor (800).

    c. Alcuin of York led the Carolingian Renaissance.

3. Three Reasons Why the Church Split

    a. One word added to a creed

        i. Western Christians added the word *filioque* ("and the Son") to the Nicene Creed; Eastern Christians objected.

    b. A bull on a communion table

        i. The bishop of Constantinople refused to recognize Pope Leo IX; In response, the pope had an insulting papal bull laid on the communion table in the Church of Holy Wisdom in Constantinople (1054).

    c. A tragic sack of an ancient city

        i. Pope Urban II called for a Crusade against Muslims in the Holy Land (1095).

        ii. Peter the Hermit caused trouble in Constantinople.

        iii. Western Crusaders sacked Constantinople in the Fourth Crusade (1204).

Key Terms

Carolingian Renaissance – Charlemagne's initiative, overseen by the monk Alcuin of York, to preserve and to spread classical learning through monasteries.

Council of Nicaea, Second (AD 787) – Seventh and last church-wide council concluded that veneration of two-dimensional icons does not violate the biblical command against graven images.

Crusades – Series of military expeditions launched by European Christians against Muslims to conquer the Holy Land. Pope Urban II called for the First Crusade in 1095. Four years later in 1099, the First Crusade conquered Jerusalem, slaughtering thousands of Jews and Muslims in the city. The Crusades lasted into the thirteenth century.

Filioque – Latin word meaning "and the Son" which Western Christians added to the Nicene Creed in the AD 800s, so that the creed indicated that the Holy Spirit proceeded from the Father *and the Son.* Eastern Christians objected to this addition, citing the church's agreement not to alter the Nicene Creed as established in the Council of Ephesus four centuries earlier.

Icons – Image of a biblical character or a sacred individual in church history, created for the purpose of religious veneration.

Iconoclasts – Those who destroy icons. They were "icon-smashers" and saw all reverence for icons as idolatry.

Iconodules – Those who revere icons. They were "icon-kissers" and saw reverence for icons as a way of remembering and rejoicing in how God had worked through past believers.

Papal Bull – A decree issued by the bishop of Rome. "Bulla" referred to the lead seal, with the pope's name on one side and the images of Peter and Paul on the other, that popes used to prevent anyone from tampering with the decree.

Roman Catholic and Eastern Orthodox Comparison

	Roman Catholicism	Eastern Orthodoxy
Name	"Catholic" means "worldwide" or "universal."	"Orthodoxy" means "correct belief" or "correct worship" and implies faithfulness to the church's ancient teachings and traditions.
Structure	The bishop or overseer of Rome is the father ("pope") over all churches. He represents Christ's leadership in the church. Overseers ("bishops") guide each region and are responsible directly to the pope. High overseers ("archbishops") are highly esteemed by other bishops, but they have no power outside their own regions. Since 1150, bishops and archbishops who advise the pope have been known as "cardinal" overseers.	Today, the Orthodox Church consists of several self-ruling groups of churches. A metropolitan patriarch ("city father") guides each group of churches. Some patriarchs also serve as high overseers ("archbishops"). Orthodox Christians highly esteem the patriarch of Constantinople (modern Istanbul, Turkey). Yet he has little official authority beyond his own churches.
Authority	Scripture as interpreted and expounded through church councils, church tradition, and bishops in union with the pope.	The teachings of the apostles as understood through the Scriptures, the first seven church-wide councils, and the ancient church fathers.

Before the Gathering

- In the *Christian History Made Easy* handbook, read chapter 5.

- Preview the video segment Session 5 and PowerPoint® presentation chapter 5.

- Study Ephesians 4:11–16 and 1 Peter 3:15–17. Incorporate in your notes and discussion a few facts that you learned from this study.

- Complete the lesson in the Participant Guide for this session.

- If you will be using the video or PowerPoint® presentation, ensure that components are connected and tested beforehand.

- Locate the article "Why is the Muslim World So Resistant to the Gospel?" at www.albertmohler.com. Print a copy of the article for each participant.

- Pray for guidance as you lead this session.

Goals for the Gathering

Through this session, participants will be able to:

- Understand the causes for the split between Roman Catholicism and Eastern Orthodoxy.

- Explain the meaning of speaking the truth in love, and keeping an attitude of meekness during disagreement.

- Identify areas to live more fully in light of the gospel when interacting with people with whom they disagree.

Get Them Talking   (10 minutes)

Read Ephesians 4:11–16 and 1 Peter 3:15–17. Scripture instructs us to speak with gentleness, not only to believers but also among non-believers. Consider the following questions and statements for group discussion:

- In Ephesians, Paul is addressing how Christians should interact with fellow Christians; in 1 Peter, Peter is considering how Christians should speak to the world. What should be similar in both of these circumstances? [Gentle and respectful attitude, because we can rest fully in what God has already accomplished through the gospel.] What should be different? [Among Christians, the goal is unity and maturity through centeredness in Jesus Christ; when speaking to non-Christians, the goal is faithful articulation of the gospel to provide opportunity for the Holy Spirit to work faith in their hearts.]

- Consider together a particular group of people who claim the title "Christian" but, because of false beliefs about Jesus, has probably never trusted Jesus. How can Christians speak the truth to them with "gentleness and respect"? (1 Peter 3:15)

- Consider a difference of opinion in your fellowship of churches or in your local church. How can the participants in your group speak "truth in love" in this situation? (Eph. 4:15).

Take a Closer Look   (30 to 60 minutes)

Watch the video segment Session 5. (25 minutes)

Optional: Review the content of the video using the PowerPoint® presentation chapter 5. (35 minutes)

Seek the Central Truth   (10 minutes)

Sometimes what is done in the name of Christ is not simply questionable—it is outright sin. That was the case when it came to the Fourth Crusade. Knights who claimed the name of Christ slaughtered and violated men, women, and children as they fought to take Constantinople. The blood that ran through the streets of Constantinople would eventually be rinsed away; the memory of the event, unfortunately, would not be so quickly washed from people's minds. "How shall I begin to tell of the deeds wrought by these nefarious men!" an eyewitness recalled. "All the most heinous sins and crimes were committed by all with equal zeal."

Anytime a Christian refuses to respond in love, the conflict—whether with Christians or with non-Christians—may be less bloody than the Fourth Crusade but it holds just as much destructive potential. Remember what James said to Christians in the first century? "What causes quarrels and what causes fights among you? Is it not this, that your passions are at war within you? You desire and do not have, so you murder. You covet and cannot obtain, so you fight and quarrel" (James 4:1–2). In the thirteenth century, warring passions led to fights, quarrels, and the tragic sack of an ancient city. Today, warring passions lead to divisions in the church and to a weakened witness among non-believers. Whenever a desire to be proven right eclipses Christ-like gentleness and humility, division and destruction are sure to follow.

James also provides a message of hope for those who have trusted Jesus. Because of the Spirit's power within us, we are able to respond to the gospel by submitting "to God" (James 4:7). Then, the devil "will flee from you. Draw near to God, and he will draw near to you" (4:8).

Possible Conflict Situation	Scriptural Response
I disagree with a brother or sister in Christ.	Eph. 4:1–16; Col. 3:12–17
A brother or sister in Christ is sinning.	Matt. 18:16–20; 1 Cor. 6:1–8; Gal. 6:1–5
I am speaking with someone who claims to be a Christian but who denies essential beliefs.	Titus 3:1–11; 1 Peter 3:15–17
I am speaking with someone who isn't a Christian at all.	Matt. 28:16–20; 1 Peter 3:15–17

Together: Look at the article "Why Is the Muslim World So Resistant to the Gospel?" How can Christians interact with Muslims with "gentleness and respect"? (1 Peter 3:15)

Wrap It Up   (5 minutes)

End your time together with a prayer similar to this one: "God our Father, help us to respond more completely to what you have already accomplished for us through Jesus Christ, the ultimate example of powerful meekness and righteous love. Grant us compassion toward others. Work in us, through your Spirit, the capacity to rest in your righteousness even in times of conflict. In the name of Jesus Christ our Lord, Amen."

Strongly encourage class members to complete the Participant Guide activities for this week.

Optional: Pray together as a group for persecuted Christians or, if time is short, ask participants to commit to praying at least once in the coming week for a specific region or country where our brothers and sisters face persecution.

Work Together

The types of disagreements that began among Christians centuries ago continue today among neighboring denominations. Serve your community this week by showing the love of Christ to a congregation of Christians from a different denomination. Consider mailing a card of encouragement to the pastor or even sending some flowers to the church. Or, have your group meet briefly with the neighboring church to pray for their congregation.

SESSION 6
God's Work Goes On

AD *500–1300*

The church in the Middle Ages was mired in corruption and controversy. Looking back, it can sometimes seem like proclamation of the gospel was completely lost. Yet was it? During this era, missionaries like Cyril and Methodius spread the message of Jesus to unreached lands. Scholars like Thomas Aquinas changed the way people looked at God's creation. Monks like Bernard of Clairvaux called people to a radical love for God, and Peter Waldo laid the foundations for future reforms. Despite the failures of his people, God's work rolled on.

Session 6 Outline

1. Missionaries

   a. Boniface and Lioba became missionaries to the Germans (716).

   b. Brothers Cyril and Methodius became missionaries to Slavic peoples (862).

2. Reformers

   a. Berno established a monastery at Cluny that sparked a revival (910).

   b. Bernard of Clairvaux called people to a deeper love of God (1115).

3. Mendicants

   a. Peter Waldo and the "poor folk" challenged church authority (1179).

   b. Francis of Assisi took a vow of poverty (1205).

4. Dominicans

   a. Thomas Aquinas brought together Aristotle's philosophy and Catholic theology in his *Summa Theologica* (1266).

Key Terms

Abbot – (from *abba*, "father") Leader in a monastic community, particularly a community that follows the Rule of Benedict.

Dominican Order – Order of Friars Preachers, founded by Dominic in the thirteenth century. Dominicans have a strong intellectual history and include notable figures such as Thomas Aquinas and Bartolome de las Casas.

Franciscans – Order of Friars Minor, founded by Francis of Assisi in the early thirteenth century. Many Franciscans have been traveling monks who model the life of Francis, including wearing plain brown robes and ropes around their waists like Francis did.

Friar – (from French, *frère*, "brother") Member of a Roman Catholic mendicant order.

Mendicants – (Latin, "beggar") Order of monks who preach, own no property, and serve the poor.

Monastery – Also known as an Abbey, the place of residence for communities of nuns or monks.

Pontiff or pontifex – (from Latin, "high priest") Beginning in the Middle Ages, a title for the bishop of Rome.

Purgatory – Roman Catholic teaching about an intermediate state of death where souls can be purged of sins and thereby become ready to enter heaven.

Scholasticism – Method for reasoning that arose in Middle Ages and tried to bring together Christian theology and Greek philosophy.

Waldensians – Also known as the Poor Folk of Lyons, they were followers of Peter Waldo in France in the twelfth century. They were persecuted for preaching without the authorization of the Roman Catholic Church.

Before the Gathering

- In the *Christian History Made Easy* handbook, read chapter 6.

- Preview the video segment Session 6 and PowerPoint® presentation chapter 6.

- Study Genesis 50:20; John 5:17; and, 2 Corinthians 12:7–10. Incorporate in your notes and discussion a few facts that you learned from this study.

- Complete the lesson in the Participant Guide for this session.

- If you will be using the video or PowerPoint® slideshow presentation, ensure that components are connected and tested beforehand.

- Locate the articles "Bernard of Clairvaux," "A Prophet without Honor," and "Thomas Aquinas" at www.christianhistory.net. Print a copy of each article for each participant.

- Pray for guidance as you lead this session.

Goals for the Gathering

Through this session, participants will be able to:

- Understand that God is always at work, even in difficult circumstances.

- Identify historical and biblical examples of how God used difficult contexts and even sinful circumstances to work out his will in the world.

- Consider how God is at work in their own lives.

Get Them Talking   (10 minutes)

Read Genesis 50:20, John 5:17, and, 2 Corinthians 12:7–10. Consider the following questions and statements for group discussion:

- How did God work in the life of Joseph to accomplish his good purpose? What specific good purposes did God accomplish through the circumstances of Joseph's life? [God's ultimate purpose in the life of Joseph was to preserve the children of Israel through whom he would bring Jesus into the world.]

- In John 5:17, Jesus declared that his Father had always been at work and that his own purpose was to do his Father's will. Describe a situation in your own life when it was difficult to remember that God is working through every circumstance.

- How did God work through Paul's circumstances in 2 Corinthians 12:7–10? [God used the sufferings of Paul to reveal the strength of his grace and the sufficiency of the cross.]

- Immediately before being martyred by a band of robbers, a missionary monk named Boniface spoke these words to his companions who were about to die alongside him: "Take comfort in the Lord and endure with gladness the suffering he has mercifully ordained. Put your faith in him and he will grant deliverance to your souls." Why can Christians endure suffering "with gladness"? [Emphasize the sufficiency of Jesus' suffering on the cross to provide assurance of God's goodness in our own times of suffering.]

Take a Closer Look   (30 to 60 minutes)

Watch the video segment Session 6. (30 minutes)

Optional: Review the content of the video using the PowerPoint® presentation chapter 6. (30 minutes)

Seek the Central Truth   (15 minutes)

God used the sin of Joseph's brothers to preserve the people through whom Jesus would be brought into the world. God worked through the cross to accomplish salvation for all who would trust in Jesus. God used the sufferings of Paul to reveal the strength of his grace and the sufficiency of the cross. And, despite the corruption and doctrinal decline in many established churches during the Middle Ages, God worked in and around these churches so that the truth about Jesus was preserved and proclaimed.

Together: Give participants the articles "Bernard of Clairvaux," "A Prophet without Honor," and "Thomas Aquinas." Organize the participants into three groups. Assign one of the articles to each group. Ask each group to work together to find in their assigned article at least one unlikely event that God used to bring glory to himself. Allow the participants ten minutes, then gather the class and discuss their findings.

Wrap It Up (5 minutes)

End your time together with a prayer similar to this one: "God, you never stop working! For that reason, we praise you. God, you have already accomplished in Jesus Christ all that is necessary for the salvation of your people! For that provision, we thank you. And yet, God, you choose to work through us! For that gift, we are amazed and we stand in awe of you. Amen."

Strongly encourage class members to complete the Participant Guide activities for this week.

Optional: Pray together as a group for persecuted Christians or, if time is short, ask participants to commit to praying at least once in the coming week for a specific region or country where our brothers and sisters face persecution.

Work Together

Look for an opportunity to join in God's work this week. Volunteer as a group to serve a meal to the homeless in your community or to provide necessities for a family that has recently lost their possessions. During your time of service, encourage these families to trust in God, but also become the means by which God's grace is revealed in their lives. Pray with and for them, that God would meet their needs and that they would trust him not only to provide their needs, but also to rescue them from sin through the gospel.

SESSION 7
Everything Falls Apart
AD *1300–1500*

Enormous tragedies in the fourteenth and fifteenth centuries challenged people's trust in God. Three popes at once vied for the papacy, the Hundred Years' War and the Black Death took millions of lives across Europe, and Muslim Turks conquered what was left of the Eastern Empire.

But in the midst of this, God raised up fresh voices, like John Wycliffe in England and Jan Hus in Bohemia, to turn people's minds to the Scriptures and the beauty of the gospel. A renaissance in learning was sparked by classical manuscripts and Gutenberg's printing press. Seeds of reform had been planted and were about to take root among God's people.

Session 7 Outline

1. Popes away from Rome

    a. Pope Boniface VIII issued the "Unam Sanctum" (1302).

    b. Popes resided near French border for 72 years (1305–1377).

2. The Hundred Years' War (1337–1453)

3. The Plague (Black Death) (mid-1300s)

4. Corruption and Division

    a. Catherine of Siena convinced the pope to return to Rome (1377).

    b. Two popes elected: One in Rome and a French pope in Avignon (1378).

    c. Council of Pisa resulted in three popes (1409).

5. Renewal of Gospel Proclamation

    a. John Wycliffe translated the Bible into English (1382).

    b. Jan Hus in Bohemia challenged the Roman Catholic Church's authority.

    c. Council of Constance burned Hus at the stake, burned Wycliffe's bones, and established one pope (1414–1418).

6. Renewal in Classical Learning

    a. Ottoman Turks conquered Constantinople (1453); Classical texts from Constantinople taken to the West.

    b. Renaissance humanism

    c. Gutenberg's printing press (1440)

    d. Erasmus' Greek New Testament (1516)

Key Terms

Council of Constance (1414–1418) – Deposed the three popes who claimed the title and elected a new pope, ending the papal schism; declared Jan Hus a heretic and burned him at the stake; declared the late John Wycliffe a heretic and burned his remains.

Council of Pisa (1409) – Deposed the two popes that claimed the title and elected a third pope. However the legitimacy of this council was disputed and the popes refused to give up their title, thus resulting in three popes. This paved the way for the Council of Constance a few years later.

Babylonian Captivity of the Church – Also called "Babylonian Captivity of the Papacy," refers to the 72 years in the fourteenth century in which the popes resided not in Rome, but in France. It began in 1305 when Clement V was elected pope but refused to move to Rome, and instead stayed in Avignon, France. It ended in 1377 when Pope Gregory XI returned to Rome at the urging of Catherine of Siena.

Humanists – Instead of emphasizing theoretical knowledge, humanists during the Renaissance emphasized practical engagement in the civic life of their communities. They valued the study of grammar, public speaking, history, poetry, and philosophy. Notable humanists included Francesco Petrarch, Leonardo da Vinci, and Desiderius Erasmus.

Hundred Years' War (1337–1453) – War between England and France in which the French eventually succeeded in expelling the English from France, but only after more than 100 years of bloody battles. The French peasant girl Joan of Arc lead several successful battles for France in this war.

Renaissance – Revival of ancient classical learning and art, beginning in the fourteenth and fifteenth centuries. Renaissance humanism emphasized practical learning and challenged the Scholasticism of the Middle Ages which focused on theoretical knowledge.

Scholasticism – Method for reasoning that arose in Middle Ages and tried to bring together Christian theology and Greek philosophy, particularly the philosophy of Aristotle. Some of the primary Scholastic thinkers were Anselm of Canterbury, Peter Abelard, and Thomas Aquinas.

Unam Sanctum (1302) – (Latin, "the one holy") A papal bull issued by Pope Boniface VIII which lays out the position of the pope as the supreme head of the church and the necessity of belonging to the church in order to have eternal salvation.

Before the Gathering

- In the *Christian History Made Easy* handbook, read chapter 7.

- Preview the video segment Session 7 and PowerPoint® presentation chapter 7.

- Study Deuteronomy 31:6, Joshua 1:5, Hebrews 13:5–6, Philippians 2:5–11, and Philippians 4:10–13. Incorporate into your notes and discussion a few facts that you learned from this study.

- Complete the lesson in the Participant Guide for this session.

- If you will be using the video or PowerPoint® presentation, ensure that components are connected and tested beforehand.

- Locate the articles "John Wycliffe," "Gutenberg: A God's-Eye View," and "Erasmus' Revolutionary 'Study Bible'" at www.christianhistory.net. Print a copy of each article for each participant.

- Pray for guidance as you lead this session.

Goals for the Gathering

Through this session, participants will be able to:

- Discuss struggles within the church and society during the fourteenth and fifteenth centuries.

- Identify examples in their own lives when situations were difficult but God's presence was clear.

- Recognize God's sovereignty over triumphs and troubles throughout history.

Get Them Talking   (10 minutes)

Read Deuteronomy 31:6, Joshua 1:5, and Hebrews 13:5–6. Consider the following questions and statements for group discussion:

- What do these Scripture verses tell us about God's presence?

- Describe a time when you were strongly aware of God's presence with you.

- Suppose your Christian friend says to you, "I don't sense God's presence anymore, and I've felt this way for a long time. How can I know that he's really there?" What answer would you offer? [Guide the participants to rely less on their own feelings of God's presence and to rely more on the fact that God has revealed his commitment to his people once and for all through the death and resurrection of Jesus and through the sending of his Spirit; God's work in past history reveals that he does not leave or forsake his people, even when his people do not feel his presence in their present circumstances.]

- Read Philippians 2:5–11; 4:10–13. How can Christians be content even in times of despair? [Guide the participants to recognize that it is through the sacrifice and resurrection triumph of Jesus that Christians receive strength to endure and to find contentment in every circumstance.]

Take a Closer Look   (30 to 60 minutes)

Watch the video segment Session 7. (25 minutes)

Optional: Review the content of the video using the PowerPoint® presentation chapter 7. (35 minutes)

Seek the Central Truth   (15 minutes)

God promised Moses and Joshua that he would never forsake his people. This same God demonstrated through the resurrection of Jesus that he will never abandon anyone who trusts in him—even if that person is dead in a tomb! (See Acts 2:22–28; 13:32–37). That's why Paul could be content even though he wrote his letter to the Philippians while he was under house arrest. That's also why, even when considering the fateful fourteenth century, we can be certain that God did not abandon those who truly trusted him.

Together: Provide each participant with copies of the three articles, "John Wycliffe," "Gutenberg: A God's-Eye View," and "Erasmus' Revolutionary 'Study Bible.'" Organize the class into three groups. Assign each group one of the three articles. Ask each group to look together at the assigned article and to consider, how did God use the fateful events of the fourteenth and fifteenth centuries to prepare people to hear and to understand truth about himself? Allow the groups ten minutes, then ask them to share their findings.

Wrap It Up   (5 minutes)

Pray through Philippians 4:10–13. Read a verse aloud and then spend a few moments in silence together, considering the verse. Then, pray a brief response to that verse and read the next verse.

Strongly encourage class members to complete the Participant Guide activities for this week.

Optional: Pray together as a group for persecuted Christians or, if time is short, ask participants to commit to praying at least once in the coming week for a specific region or country where our brothers and sisters face persecution.

Work Together

Many people in the churches of the fourteenth century cared for disease-afflicted people. Select one or two individuals in your congregation or community who are ill. Visit them as a group this week. Sit with them. Pray with them. Read Scripture with them. Ask them what needs your church may be able to fulfill in their lives.

SESSION 8
The Reformation
AD *1500–1600*

So many influences came together in the sixteenth century to bring about gospel renewal in Europe. Wycliffe and Hus had packed a powder keg. Erasmus had woven a fuse. On October 31, 1517, a hotheaded monk named Martin Luther lit the fuse and rocked the world.

Soon after, other reformers, like John Calvin and William Tyndale, in defiance of church and state authorities didn't let up in their mission to spread the Word of God to peasant and noble alike. Meanwhile, a radical group known as the Anabaptists arose and began to press the limits even further.

Session 8 Outline

1. How reformation began with the righteousness of God.

    a. Martin Luther:

        i.   Became a monk and sought righteousness (Ps. 31:1; Rom. 1:17).
        ii. Posted 95 Theses to protest the sale of indulgences (October 31, 1517).
        iii. Defended his writings at the Diet of Worms (1521).

    b. John Calvin wrote *Institutes of the Christian Religion* in Geneva, Switzerland.

    c. Ulrich Zwingli challenged church practices in Zurich, Switzerland.

2. How reformation turned radical.

    a. Anabaptist Felix Manz became the first Protestant martyred by other Protestants (1527).

    b. Menno Simons led a group of Anabaptists who later became known as Mennonites.

3. How reformation reached England.

    a. William Tyndale translated the New Testament into common English (1525).

4. How reformation looked in the Roman Catholic Church.

    a. Colloquy of Regensburg failed to unify Catholics and Protestants (1541).

    b. Ignatius Loyola founded the Society of Jesus (Jesuit Order).

    c. Council of Trent (1545–1563):

        i.   Denied justification by faith alone.
        ii. Affirmed that the elements of the Lord's Supper become the body and blood of Jesus Christ.
        iii. Proclaimed that the Bible is to be interpreted according to and with church tradition.

Key Terms

Anabaptists – (from Greek, "again-baptizer") They taught—contrary to infant baptism—that only believers should be baptized ("believers' baptism"). Mennonites, Quakers, and the Amish have their roots in the Anabaptist movement.

Colloquy of Regensburg (1541) – Conference held in Regensburg, Germany to bring Protestants and Catholics together. But after weeks of theological debate, the conference ended in a stalemate.

Council of Trent (1545–1563) – After the failed attempt at unity in the Colloquy of Regensburg, the Catholic Church at the Council of Trent formally rejected Protestant teachings.

Indulgences – In Roman Catholic theology, it's a release from the temporal (earthly) penalties that a person must endure to demonstrate repentance from his or her sins.

Jesuit Order – Religious order founded by Ignatius of Loyola in the sixteenth century. Today, Jesuits are one of the largest religious orders of the Catholic Church. They are known for their missionary work, social justice, and colleges and universities.

Lutherans – Protestant denomination emerging from the work of Martin Luther in the sixteenth century. Lutherans today number more than 60 million worldwide.

Mennonites – Anabaptist group founded by Menno Simons in the sixteenth century. Today, Mennonites are the largest of the Anabaptist groups. They are sometimes known as "peace churches" because of their emphasis on non-violence and pacifism.

Protestants – Groups during the Reformation that rejected the supreme authority of the pope later became known as Protestants. Today, Protestants include denominations such as Lutherans, Presbyterians, Anglicans, and many others.

Purgatory – Roman Catholic teaching about an intermediate state of death where souls can be purged of sins and thereby become ready to enter heaven.

Solas – (from Latin, "alone") Five statements that summarize the Reformation understanding of salvation: *sola fide* (salvation is through faith alone), *sola gratia* (salvation is by God's grace alone), *sola Scriptura* (written witness to God's way of salvation is Scripture alone), *solus Christus* (salvation is in Christ alone), *soli Deo gloria* (salvation is for God's glory alone).

Transubstantiation – In Roman Catholic teaching, transubstantiation is a way of explaining how Christ is truly present in the bread and wine of the Lord's Supper. The substance of the elements—which is invisible—becomes the blood and body of Jesus, while the visible things of the elements—such as shape, taste, color, texture—remain unchanged.

Before the Gathering

- In the *Christian History Made Easy* handbook, read chapter 8.

- Preview the video segment Session 8 and PowerPoint® presentation chapter 8.

- Study Acts 15:35–41; 16:4–5; Galatians 1:6–9; 2:11–14. Incorporate into your notes and discussion a few facts that you learned from this study.

- Complete the lesson in the Participant Guide for this session.

- If you will be using the video or PowerPoint® presentation, ensure that components are connected and tested beforehand.

- Pray for guidance as you lead this session.

Goals for the Gathering

Through this session, participants will be able to:

- Identify the primary leaders and events of the Reformation.

- Identify three types of conflict in the church.

- Consider how God may use conflicts to multiply his mission.

Get Them Talking (10 minutes)

Read Acts 15:35–41; 16:4–5; Galatians 1:6–9; 2:11–14. Consider the following questions and statements for group discussion:

- From these Bible verses, three types of conflicts can be observed:

  1. Conflict between Christians over an issue of how best to accomplish God's mission (Acts 15:35–41; 16:4–5)

  2. Conflict between Christians over an issue of sin or acting in a way that is not in line with biblical truth (Gal. 2:11–14)

  3. Conflict between Christians and people who claim to be Christians but who have denied the gospel (Gal. 1:6–9)

- How should Christians deal differently with each of these three types of conflict?

- How did God work through the conflict that separated Paul and Barnabas? [Their separation resulted in two mission teams instead of only one, Acts 15:39–41.]

- What was Paul's perspective on John Mark near the end of Paul's earthly life? [John Mark became a valued companion of Paul; Col. 4:10; Philem. 1:24; 2 Tim. 4:11.]

Take a Closer Look   (30 to 60 minutes)

Watch the video segment Session 8. (35 minutes)

Optional: Review the content of the video using the PowerPoint® presentation chapter 8. (25 minutes)

Seek the Central Truth   (15 minutes)

Disagreements happen! Paul disagreed with Barnabas over John Mark, Paul confronted Peter (known in Galatians by his Aramaic name, Cephas) over eating with non-Jews, and Paul clashed with unnamed teachers in Galatia who claimed that Gentiles who truly trusted Jesus must also keep the Jewish law. Yet God worked even through these disagreements. Paul's clashes with false teachers led to a clear articulation of the gospel in his letter to the Galatians. Paul's confrontation with Peter made it clear to all that God's plan included both Jews and non-Jews.

The disagreement between Paul and Barnabas led to a multiplication of God's mission. This is not to suggest that sin or heresy is excusable! It is, instead, to recognize that God works even through human failures.

In the sixteenth century, disagreements ripped apart the established church. Yet God used these disagreements to multiply his mission throughout the world.

Together: List as many conflicts as you can recall that occurred during the sixteenth-century Reformation. Then, review the three types of conflict. Determine which of the three categories best describes each of the conflicts that occurred during the Reformation.

Wrap It Up (5 minutes)

End your time together with a prayer similar to this one: "God, so many conflicts still separate your people from one another. Make us both humble and strong: strong to stand for your truth, but humble so that we never stand for our own sakes or in our own strength. Bring us together for the sake of your mission. In the name of Jesus Christ, our Lord and the head of the church, Amen."

Strongly encourage class members to complete the Participant Guide activities for this week.

Optional: Pray together as a group for persecuted Christians or, if time is short, ask participants to commit to praying at least once in the coming week for a specific region or country where our brothers and sisters face persecution.

Work Together

For centuries prior to the Reformation, many church leaders saw marriage, childbearing, and adoption as necessary evils. The Reformers recognized anew the goodness of these gifts. Martin Luther saw the family as "a school for character"—a God-ordained context for Christian formation and discipleship. In your group, help one another to make plans for effective family devotional times during the upcoming week. If one or more group members are single and have no children, provide opportunities for them to be included in one or more family devotional times this week.

SESSION 9
Post-Reformation Growing Pains
AD *1600–1700*

The seventeenth century was an era in flux. The church had fractured into a myriad of Protestant groups across Europe. The new congregations struggled over theological issues like predestination, infant baptism, and the relationship between church and state. Puritans wanted to purify the Church of England, while Separatists left and started their own congregations.

Though discovery of the Americas opened up possibilities to spread the gospel, the New World quickly became marred by the exploitation of natives and the importation of African slaves. Courageous believers like Bartolome de las Casas and William Wilberforce would spend their lives fighting these terrible injustices.

Session 9 Outline

1. Clashes between Protestants and Catholics

    a. Defenestration of Prague (1618)

    b. Thirty Years' War (1618–1648)

2. Clashes among Protestants

    a. Jacob Arminius disputed Calvinism's view of predestination.

    b. Synod of Dort sided with Calvinism (1618).

3. Conflicts in England

    a. Puritans tried to purify the Church of England by presenting the Millenary Petition to King James I (1603).

    b. King James Bible was published (1611).

    c. Westminster Assembly was called to restructure the Church of England (1643–1649).

    d. Oliver Cromwell allowed different Christian groups to worship freely.

    e. Separatists

        i.   John Smyth led the first English Baptists.
        ii. John Bunyan wrote *The Pilgrim's Progress* (1678).

4. Clashes in the New World

    a. Bartolome de las Casas campaigned against the encomienda system (1545).

    b. Pedro Claver, "always a slave to Africans" (1622).

    c. William Wilberforce worked to abolish the British slave trade.

Key Terms

Arminianism – (named for Jacob Arminius) Belief that God gives every human being the gift (known as "prevenient grace") of being able to decide on their own whether to trust Jesus when they hear the gospel. God foresaw which individuals would choose to trust Jesus, and God planned in eternity past to save and to regenerate those individuals in response to their choice to trust Jesus.

Baptists – Christians who accept baptism of believers only and who view each local congregation of believers as autonomous. John Smyth (1570–1612) is often considered the first English Baptist.

Calvinism – (named for John Calvin; also called Reformed theology) Belief that, because human beings are dead in their sins, no one will choose to trust Jesus for salvation unless they are first regenerated ("born again") by God's Spirit. God planned in eternity past ("predestined") to regenerate particular individuals. When those who are predestined are born anew and hear the gospel, they respond to God's work in their lives by trusting Jesus for salvation.

Defenestration of Prague (1618) – An assembly of Protestants in Prague concluded that Roman Catholic leaders were guilty of closing Protestant churches in Bohemia. At the assembly, the Protestants threw the Catholic envoys out the window. Although the Catholic envoys survived the fall, this incident was one of several events that triggered the Thirty Years' War between Catholics and Protestants.

Encomienda System – The exploitation of natives on plantations in the Americas, particularly by the Spanish settlers.

Hampton Court Conference (1604) – Meeting between King James I of England and the Puritans in response to the Millenary Petition. Puritan concerns about English Bible translations discussed at this conference led to King James I calling for a new translation of the Bible; this translation later became known as the King James Version.

King James Bible (1611) – Also called the Authorized Version, King James I of England initiated this translation in 1604 after the Hampton Court Conference. The translation was completed in 1611 and became the standard Bible used in the Church of England.

Millenary Petition (1603) – Letter signed by 1,000 Puritan leaders given to King James I of England requesting, among other items: (1) simpler Sunday worship services in the Book of Common Prayer, (2) pastors that were "able and sufficient" preachers, (3) bishops to be no longer provided with multiple residences, and (4) church discipline administered according to New Testament.

Puritans – Protestants in sixteenth- and seventeenth-century England who wanted to purify the Church of England by reviving New Testament patterns of worship. Some Puritans from England sailed to America and settled the Massachusetts Bay Colony around the year 1630.

Separatists – Protestants in sixteenth- and seventeenth-century England who separated from the Church of England and formed independent congregations. One group of Separatists, originally from England, sailed to America and founded Plymouth Colony in Massachusetts in 1620.

Synod of Dort (1618) – Assembly of the Reformed Church in Dort, Netherlands that addressed the issue of Arminianism. The assembly rejected Arminianism and produced the *Canons of Dort* outlining Reformed (Calvinist) beliefs.

Thirty Years' War (1618–1648) – A conflict primarily between Protestant nations and Roman Catholic nations, beginning with the Defenestration of Prague and ending with the Peace of Westphalia.

Westminster Assembly (1643–1649) – Gathering of church leaders in England to reorganize the Church of England. The assembly produced the *Westminster Confession of Faith* in 1646.

Before the Gathering

- In the *Christian History Made Easy* handbook, read chapter 9.

- Preview the video segment Session 9 and PowerPoint® presentation chapter 9.

- Study 2 Timothy 2:14–3:17. Incorporate in your notes and discussion a few facts that you learned from this study.

- Complete the lesson in the Participant Guide for this session.

- Carefully study the chart in this Leader Guide that contrasts Calvinism and Arminianism.

- Refer again to the article "A Call for Theological Triage and Christian Maturity" from www.albertmohler.com (see "Before the Gathering" in Session 2). Print a copy of this article for every participant.

- If you will be using the video or PowerPoint® presentation, ensure that components are connected and tested beforehand.

- Pray for guidance as you lead this session.

Goals for the Gathering

Through this session, participants will be able to:

- Compare and contrast Arminianism and Calvinism.

- Determine what it means to hold true to sound doctrine.

- Consider how they can respond biblically to incorrect teachings.

Get Them Talking (10 minutes)

Organize into three groups. Assign each group one of the following three passages to discuss: 2 Timothy 2:14–26; 3:1–9; 3:10–17. After five minutes, bring the groups back together and have each group share what was learned. Consider the following questions for discussion after the groups re-gather:

- Paul said not to quarrel about words (2 Tim. 2:14), but Paul also clearly called for the removal of certain church members who were teaching incorrect perspectives on God (2:17–26). Paul did not intend for church members to avoid quarrels by overlooking false teachings! Instead, Paul's point was that, if the individual persisted in false teachings even after being warned, he or she should be lovingly removed from church membership with the hope that he or she will repent (2:26). What process did Jesus provide for removing persons who sin against the community by remaining in persistent sin or by refusing to stop teaching heresy? [See Matthew 18:15–20. Consider also 1 Corinthians 5:1–12; 2 Corinthians 2:5–11.]

- How can churches determine which beliefs call for church discipline, if they are denied? [Refer to the idea of theological triage. First-order beliefs are so essential that to deny them is to reject the Christian faith; clearly, denial of these beliefs calls for church discipline. Differences over second-order beliefs mean that it will be difficult to remain in the same local church; second-order differences do not, however, mean that someone should be treated as a non-believer. Third-order differences should be accepted as part of the beautiful diversity that God has brought together in the local church; Paul described how to respond to third-order issues in Romans 14.]

- According to Hebrews 1:2, the "last days" began when God sent Jesus to earth. From that point until the end of time, it will be necessary for Christians to guard against the practices that Paul described in 2 Timothy 3:2–4. What should the church do today to guard against such patterns of life?

- According to 2 Timothy 3:16–17, what provides the authoritative foundation for determining and defending the beliefs that matter most?

Take a Closer Look   (30 to 60 minutes)

Watch the video segment Session 9. (30 minutes)

Optional: Review the content of the video using the PowerPoint® presentation chapter 9. (30 minutes)

Seek the Central Truth   (15 minutes)

Consider together these four controversies in the churches:

- Bartolome de Las Casas' excommunication of encomienda owners

- Hampton Court Conference

- Defenestration of Prague

- Synod of Dort

For each controversy, discuss these two questions:

- Thinking again through the article on theological triage, did the issues involved fit best in the first order, second order, or third order?

- Did church leaders deal with the controversy in a responsible and biblical manner, considering where the issues fit best in the theological triage?

Organize the students into two groups, one to consider Calvinism and the other to consider Arminianism. Refer them to the Arminianism and Calvinism chart in their participant guides. After a few minutes, ask each group to summarize the strengths and the weaknesses of their assigned position, Calvinism or Arminianism. Be willing to discuss both perspectives with grace but do not allow arguments to arise! Simply recognize the strong and weak points of each position. Make sure to recognize that both Calvinists and Arminians can be faithful Christians who trust in God's sovereignty and who are passionate about the gospel.

Wrap It Up   (5 minutes)

End your time together with a prayer similar to this one, based on 2 Timothy 4:18: "God our Father, rescue us from every evil deed and false doctrine. Bring us safely to your heavenly kingdom through the work of Jesus Christ our Lord. Be glorified even into the ages through the work of the Spirit within us. Amen."

Strongly encourage class members to complete the Participant Guide activities for this week.

Optional: Pray together as a group for persecuted Christians or, if time is short, ask participants to commit to praying at least once in the coming week for a specific region or country where our brothers and sisters face persecution.

Work Together

Being a pastor is not an easy job! Leading a congregation through the changes and disputes that arise in churches is a challenging task. Take some time this week to show your church leaders how much you appreciate their dedication. Here are some practical ideas: offer to babysit their kids, do odd jobs around their house, give them a gift card to a Christian bookstore or their favorite restaurant, put together a fun gift basket, or send them an email or card sincerely thanking them for all they do.

Arminianism and Calvinism

Issue	Arminianism *(The Remonstrance)*	Calvinism, Reformed Theology *(The Canons of Dort)*
Predestination John 6:44; 15:16; Rom. 9:10–16	**Conditional predestination.** God observed from eternity past who would believe, then God predestined people according to this foresight. *"God, by an eternal, unchangeable purpose in Jesus Christ ... before the foundation of the world, ... determined ... to save ... those who ... shall believe on this his Son Jesus, and shall persevere." (Arminian Remonstrance, Article I)*	**Unconditional predestination.** God predestined people to be saved not because he foresaw any good choices in them but simply because of his grace. *"Before the foundation of the world, by sheer grace, ... God chose in Christ to salvation a definite number of particular people. ... This election took place, not on the basis of foreseen faith ... but rather for the purpose of faith." (Canons of Dort, I)*
Atonement Job 42:1-2; John 10:14–15, 28; 1 John 2:2	**Indefinite atonement.** Jesus obtained redemption for every human being, but these people can refuse to believe and, whenever someone does refuse, God's work of redemption is thwarted in that person's life. *"Jesus Christ ...died for all men and for every man, so that he has obtained for them all ... redemption, and the forgiveness of sins; yet that no one actually enjoys this forgiveness of sins, except the believer." (Article II)*	**Definite atonement.** Though the atoning sacrifice of Jesus was sufficient to redeem the whole world, this death purchased the salvation only of those whom God in his grace chose before time. *"This death of God's Son is ... more than sufficient to atone for the sins of the whole world. ... It was God's will that Christ through the blood of the cross ... should effectively redeem from every people, tribe, nation, and language all those and only those who were chosen from eternity to salvation and given to him by the Father." (Canons, II)*

Issue	Arminianism	Calvinism
Human Nature Ps. 14:2–3; 53:2–3; Rom. 3:10–12; Eph. 2:1–3	**Defective human nature.** Although people will not do anything good in their own power, enough grace remains in every human to choose faith in Jesus. *"Man ... of and by himself can neither think, will, nor do anything that is truly good; ... it is needful that he be born again of God in Christ, through his Holy Spirit." (Article III)*	**Radically corrupted human nature.** Humanity's fallenness is so great that no one naturally desires to submit to God or to trust in Jesus. *"All people are conceived in sin and are born children of wrath, ... neither willing nor able to return to God." (Canons, III/IV)*
Grace John 6:37, 44; Eph. 2:4–6	**Resistible grace.** When God's Spirit works in a sinner to bring about the new birth, the sinner can reject God's attempts to bring new life. *"As respects the mode of the operation of this grace, it is not irresistible, inasmuch as it is written concerning many that they have resisted the Holy Ghost." (Article IV)*	**Effective grace.** Though people do resist the Holy Spirit up to the time when God brings about new life in them, God transforms the person at the time of the new birth (or regeneration) so that he or she desires to trust Jesus and actually does believe. *"Regeneration ... is an entirely supernatural work. ... All those in whose hearts God works in this marvelous way are certainly, unfailingly, and effectively reborn and do actually believe." (Canons, III/IV)*
Perseverance John 10:27–28; Rom. 8:29–39	**Perseverance dependent on the believer's will and work.** Scripture does not clearly state whether a Christian can forfeit his or her salvation. *"Those who are incorporated into Christ, ... Jesus Christ assists them ... and, if only they are ready for the conflict, and desire his help, and are not inactive, keeps them from falling. ... Whether they are capable ... of forsaking again the first beginnings of their life in Christ, ... that must be more particularly determined out of the Holy Scriptures." (Article V)*	**Perseverance dependent on God's will and work.** God works in the lives of Christians so that they persevere in faith to the end. *"God ... does not take the Holy Spirit from his own completely, even when they fall grievously. Neither does God let them fall down so far that they forfeit the grace of adoption and the state of justification. ... God preserves, continues, and completes this work by the hearing and reading of the gospel, by meditation on it, by its exhortations, threats, and promises, and also by the use of the sacraments." (Canons, V)*

SESSION 10
Revolutions in the New World

AD *1600–1800*

Revolutionary ideas in the New World changed the way people saw the world. A small band of Pilgrims on the Mayflower, Puritans in Massachusetts, and one exiled man named Roger Williams forged different paths toward religious liberty. Meanwhile, the scientific revolution caused people to wonder, what if God merely created this machine-like world and then left us alone?

At a time when society was viewing God as increasingly distant, the Great Awakening would prove otherwise. A few unlikely men—a cross-eyed preacher named George Whitefield, a struggling missionary named John Wesley, and an unpopular gangly pastor named Jonathan Edwards—were all used by God to bring tidal waves of revival to the American colonies and beyond.

Session 10 Outline

1. Revolution in Religious Liberty

   a. "Saints" and "strangers" on the Mayflower landed in Plymouth (1620).

   b. Roger Williams founded Providence Colony on the idea of religious freedom (1636).

2. Revolution in Human Reason

   a. Isaac Newton described the universe as a machine.

   b. Deism and Enlightenment contributed to a rising focus on science and human reason as the primary means for making sense of life.

3. Revival and the Great Awakening

   a. Moravian Pietists held a 100-year prayer meeting on the estate of Nikolaus von Zinzendorf in Germany.

   b. John and Charles Wesley founded Methodism in England.

   c. Jonathan Edwards led revival in American colonies.

   d. George Whitefield preached to huge crowds in England and American colonies.

4. The American Revolution

Key Terms

Deism – Belief that God created the world but that he no longer acts directly or supernaturally in his world. Instead, he endowed the created order with natural laws that, if followed, lead to blessings.

Enlightenment – (also called the Age of Reason) Seventeenth- and eighteenth-century social and philosophical movement that emphasized reason as the primary source of authority, displacing divine revelation.

Methodist – Beginning as a Pietist movement, Methodism was established by John and Charles Wesley during the Great Awakening. Called "Methodist" because of their methodological approach to routines of prayer, fasting, Bible reading and other practices. Methodists hold to Arminian, not Calvinist views. Today, Methodists number 20–40 million worldwide.

Moravian Pietists – Also known as *Unitas Fratrum* or "Unity of the Brethren," they trace their roots back to Jan Hus in the fourteenth century. When they fled Moravia in 1722 they established the Herrnhut religious community in Saxony on the estate of Nikolaus von Zinzendorf.

Pietism – Seventeenth- and eighteenth-century Protestant movement that emphasized a life of personal discipline and devotion. The publication of *Pious Desires* by Lutheran pastor Philipp Jakob Spener marked an important beginning point for Pietism. Spener deeply influenced Nikolaus von Zinzendorf, who in turn influenced the Moravian Brothers and the Methodist movement.

Providence Colony – Colony in Rhode Island founded by Roger Williams in 1636 who defected from the Massachusetts Bay Colony. Williams established Providence with the intent of providing religious freedom.

Puritans – Protestants in sixteenth- and seventeenth-century England who wanted to purify the Church of England by reviving New Testament patterns of worship. Some Puritans from England sailed to America and settled the Massachusetts Bay Colony around the year 1630.

Revival (Great Awakening) – Revival is unusual work of God by which God applies the gospel to his people in an unusually powerful way, resulting in salvation of sinners and renewed obedience among saints. The human means through which God works to bring revival are faithful proclamation of the gospel (Rom. 10:15–17) and fervent prayer among God's people (James 5:16). The Great Awakening in the mid-1700s in Europe and the American colonies is an example of revival.

Separatists – English Protestants who separated from the Church of England and formed independent congregations. The pilgrims on the Mayflower who settled Plymouth Colony in Massachusetts were Separatists.

Before the Gathering

- In the *Christian History Made Easy* handbook, read chapter 10.

- Preview the video segment Session 10 and PowerPoint® presentation chapter 10.

- Use a concordance and trace the term "truth" throughout the Gospel of John. Focus on John 1:14–18; 14:1–7; 18:28–38. Incorporate in your notes and discussion a few facts that you learned from this study.

- Complete the lesson in the Participant Guide for this session.

- If you will be using the video or PowerPoint® presentation, ensure that components are connected and tested beforehand.

- Locate the article "Nikolaus von Zinzendorf: Christ-Centered Moravian 'Brother'" at www.christianhistory.net. Print a copy of the article for each participant.

- Pray for guidance as you lead this session.

Goals for the Gathering

Through this session, participants will be able to:

- Understand how the Enlightenment and the Great Awakening impacted Christianity.

- Consider whether they perceive Jesus as the first and central source of all truth.

Get Them Talking   (15 minutes)

Provide a brief overview of the idea of "truth" throughout the Gospel of John (see especially John 1:14–18; 14:1–7; 18:28–38). Consider the following questions and statements for group discussion:

- What is "truth" according to John's Gospel? [Emphasize the person of Jesus as the incarnation of God's truth. Remind the class that the authors of the New Testament were eyewitnesses of the risen Lord Jesus or close associates of eyewitnesses. These writers testified faithfully to the truth of Jesus.]

- Read Colossians 1:15–17. Jesus is the truth of God in human flesh and the One who brings order to the entire cosmos. What impact should these facts have on how Christians respond to knowledge gained through the sciences or other areas of study?

- What was Jesus' purpose in coming into the world? (see John 18:37)

- In light of what you have learned, what was the answer to Pontius Pilate's question in John 18:38?

Take a Closer Look (30 to 60 minutes)

Watch the video segment Session 10. (25 minutes)

Optional: Review the content of the video using the PowerPoint® presentation chapter 10. (35 minutes)

Seek the Central Truth (15 minutes)

Use the article "Nikolaus von Zinzendorf: Christ-Centered Moravian 'Brother'" to review and to learn about Pietism. What were some strengths as well as possible weaknesses of Pietism?

Return to John 14:6 and 18:38. Consider the following three types of people:

- Early scientists such as Isaac Newton

- Enlightenment rationalists and Deists

- Leaders in the Great Awakening like Jonathan Edwards and John Wesley

How might these people have answered Pilate's question, "What is truth?" (John 18:38)?

Wrap It Up (5 minutes)

End your time together with a prayer similar to this one: "Father, thank you for sending the truth to us in the person of Jesus Christ. Work in us through your Spirit so that we may see Jesus as the source of truth in whom all other truths come together. Amen."

Strongly encourage class members to complete the Participant Guide activities for this week.

Optional: Pray together as a group for persecuted Christians or, if time is short, ask participants to commit to praying at least once in the coming week for a specific region or country where our brothers and sisters face persecution.

Work Together

Many college-aged students are searching for truth! Brainstorm some ways you can reach out to a college student this week. (Hint: They love food!) Share with them something you've learned in this class. Ask them what they are learning about life and God.

SESSION 11
Ageless Faith
in an Age of Reason
AD *1800–1900*

The Enlightenment cast aside faith and religion in favor of science and reason. Faith became a private thing—whatever works for you. The question that faced Christians in this era—and still faces believers today—was, if faith is just a personal matter, how do we show that the gospel of Jesus is needed by all people?

Christians responded to this emerging secular worldview in a variety of ways: A burgeoning missions movement was led by individuals such as William Carey, revivalists like Charles Spurgeon and Dwight Moody crisscrossed Europe and North America preaching a simple gospel message, liberal theologians tried to accommodate Christianity to the modern world, and the Catholic Church doubled-down on church authority.

Session 11 Outline

1. The Enlightenment ("Age of Reason")

    a. Scientific facts and human reason

2. Challenges to Established Authorities

    a. French Revolution cast aside the Catholic Church (1793).

    b. William Carey challenged Particular Baptists and began modern missions (1792).

    c. Church influence declined while a secular worldview emerged.

3. Five Responses to the Modern World

    a. Romanticism: Friedrich Schleiermacher tried to preserve Christianity with theological liberalism.

    b. Reform: Sunday School (Robert Raikes), Temperance, Abolitionists

    c. Revivalism

        i.   Revival in Cane Ridge, Kentucky.
        ii. Barton Stone tried to end denominations.
        iii. Charles Finney's "philosophical" approach to revival.
        iv. Dwight L. Moody led evangelistic crusades.
        v.   Charles Spurgeon preached the gospel in simple ways.

    d. Resistance: First Vatican Council declared infallibility of the pope (1869).

    e. Rejecting what we must, redeeming what we can: Niagara Bible Conference of 1895 agreed on five fundamentals.

Key Terms

Abolitionism – Movement in the 1700s and 1800s to abolish the trade in African slaves.

Empiricism – Worldview that sees knowledge gained through scientific observation and the physical senses as primary, discounting knowledge gained through other sources and dismissing completely any knowledge that depends on divine revelation.

Enlightenment – (also called the Age of Reason) Seventeenth- and eighteenth-century social and philosophical movement that emphasized reason as the primary source of authority, displacing divine revelation.

First Vatican Council (1869–1870) – Over 700 Catholic bishops convened in Vatican City to deal with issues arising from modernism. Among other things, the council confirmed the infallibility of the pope as church doctrine.

Fundamentals – Beliefs that had been denied in theologically-liberal groups but which were emphasized strongly at certain Bible conferences throughout the late nineteenth and early twentieth centuries. Five of these fundamental beliefs were (1) inerrancy of Scripture, (2) deity of Jesus, (3) virgin conception of Jesus, (4) death of Jesus in place of sinners, and (5) bodily resurrection.

Industrial Revolution – Advancements in technology and transportation in the late 1700s and 1800s that shifted society from farm-based and home-based to an urban, factory-based society. Many people moved to cities to find work in factories.

Inerrancy – Belief that the inspired human authors of the Scriptures never affirmed anything contrary to fact when writing the texts that became part of the biblical canon; as a result, Christians can be confident that the Bible never errs.

Revival – A work of God by which the gospel is applied to people's lives in unusually powerful ways, resulting in salvation of sinners and renewed obedience among saints. The human means by which God brings revival are faithful proclamation of the gospel (Rom. 10:15–17) and fervent prayer among God's people (Acts 1:14; 2:42; see also Isaiah 63:15–64:12).

Revivalism – Religious movement beginning in the late eighteenth century that emphasized the use of human measures to bring about salvation and spiritual renewal. Revivalism was rooted in Nathaniel W. Taylor's New Haven theology and popularized by Charles Grandison Finney.

Romanticism – Eighteenth- and nineteenth-century reaction against Enlightenment rationalism and the Industrial Revolution; emphasized experience and emotion above reason and efficiency.

Temperance Movement – Social reform movement in the nineteenth and early twentieth centuries that promoted moderation or abstention in alcohol consumption.

Theological Liberalism – Theological movement that downplayed the authority of Scripture; theological liberals focused on the imitation of Christ's ethics and on living with a deep awareness of a divine presence in all of life. Friedrich Schleiermacher is sometimes called "the father of Protestant theological liberalism."

Five Fundamentals from the Niagara Bible Conference

Fundamental Belief	Explanation
Verbal inerrancy of Scripture	God inspired the very words of Scripture; these words, taken together, tell the truth and never err.
Deity of Christ	Jesus was and is fully God.
Virgin conception of Christ	Jesus was conceived through the power of the Holy Spirit and born of the Virgin Mary.
Vicarious expiation	On the cross, Jesus endured God's wrath against sin in place of every person who would trust in him. Also known as "substitutionary atonement."
Bodily resurrection of Jesus on the third day and of all humanity at the return of Christ	Jesus rose bodily from the grave on the third day; he will return to earth and raise to life the bodies of all humanity, both those made righteous through faith in him and those who will stand condemned.

The Two-Storied House

In the eighteenth and nineteenth centuries, people began to think in terms of a separation between the public sphere of scientific facts and reason, and the private or personal sphere of faith and values. In the minds of many people, Christian faith became relegated to private sphere and began to be seen as irrelevant to public discourse.

(Model based on Nancy Pearcey's description of the two-tiered view of truth in her book *Total Truth*.)

Before the Gathering

- In the *Christian History Made Easy* handbook, read chapter 11.

- Preview the video segment Session 11 and PowerPoint® presentation chapter 11.

- Study Matthew 28:16–20; Romans 10:14–17; 1 Corinthians 9:19–23; and, James 5:16–18. Incorporate into your notes and discussion a few facts that you learned from this study.

- Complete the lesson in the Participant Guide for this session.

- If you will be using the video or PowerPoint® presentation, ensure that components are connected and tested beforehand.

- Locate the article "Charles Finney: Father of American Revivalism" at www. christianhistory.net and "The Legacy of Charles Finney" by Michael Horton at www.modernreformation.org. Carefully study both articles. Print copies of the articles for each participant.

- Pray for guidance as you lead this session.

Goals for the Gathering

Through this session, participants will be able to:

- Understand how the modern missions movement began.

- Understand how changes in society like the Industrial Revolution and the Enlightenment impacted—and still does impact—Christianity.

- Articulate the means that God uses to bring about revival as well as the possible dangers of revivalism.

Get Them Talking   (10 minutes)

Read Matthew 28:16–20; Romans 10:14–17; 1 Corinthians 9:19–23; and, James 5:16–18. Consider the following questions and statements for group discussion:

- What human means has God ordained to bring sinners to faith in Jesus? [The gospel being proclaimed to sinners, Rom. 10:14–17]

- According to the Great Commission from Jesus (Matt. 28:19), his followers are responsible to proclaim the gospel to "all nations" or "all people groups." In his first letter to the Corinthians, Paul described how proclaiming the gospel to all people groups may require Christians to give up some of their own personal liberties. What liberties do believers today enjoy that we might give up to proclaim the gospel more effectively to particular people groups? [Consider aspects of our lives that are not sinful but which we might give up if we were called to proclaim the gospel to a particular people group where that aspect of our lives could distract people from the gospel. In some contexts, for example, certain clothes, foods, beverages, or entertainment might distract hearers from the message of Jesus.]

- "Revival" is not a series of special weeknight worship services! "Revival" describes a time when the gospel is applied to people's lives in unusually powerful ways. Revival results in salvation of sinners and renewed obedience among saints. Is it possible for human beings to cause revival in their own power? [Help students to see that revival is a work of God. Christians can proclaim the gospel faithfully and pray (Acts 1:14; 2:42; Romans 10:14–17), but God alone can bring about authentic revival.]

- What role does prayer play in fulfilling the Great Commission?

Take a Closer Look   (30 to 60 minutes)

Watch the video segment Session 11. (35 minutes)

Optional: Review the content of the video using the PowerPoint® presentation chapter 11. (25 minutes)

Seek the Central Truth   (15 minutes)

Discuss the differences between "revival" and "revivalism" (see Key Terms). Distribute and discuss the two articles about Charles Finney. Help participants to see the potential danger of revivalism: When Christians become convinced that certain human measures or methods can cause revival, we have neglected the truth that God alone brings authentic revival.

Wrap It Up   (5 minutes)

End your time together with a prayer similar to this one: "Father, how deeply we desire your name to be glorified in the languages and rhythms of every people group! Show us our role in proclaiming the gospel of your Son among all the nations. Move in these nations by your Spirit to bring true and lasting revival. Amen."

Strongly encourage class members to complete the Participant Guide activities for this week.

Optional: Pray together as a group for persecuted Christians or, if time is short, ask participants to commit to praying at least once in the coming week for a specific region or country where our brothers and sisters face persecution.

Work Together

As a group, study a map of your area and choose a "mission field" in your own community. Engage in a prayer-walk this area of your community. In the prayer-walk, simply walk two-by-two throughout the area, praying fervently for revival as you walk. Afterward, make specific plans to meet some neighbors in this area. Be alert for opportunities to serve people and to speak the gospel with faithfulness and clarity.

SESSION 12
A Global Gospel
AD *1900–Present*

In the early twentieth century, many people were optimistic that all Christian groups—from Catholics to Protestants and fundamentalists to liberals—could be brought together to reach the world with the gospel. But what is the gospel? Every generation must answer that question. Evangelists like Billy Graham, theologians like Karl Barth, and trailblazers like Dietrich Bonhoeffer sought to articulate the gospel message for their generation.

In the twenty-first century, we too must continue that same mission of communicating the gospel, and stand firmly on the assurance that whatever the future holds, God will always be faithful to preserve his church.

Session 12 Outline

1. Twentieth-Century Optimism

   a. Holiness Movement; Charles Fox Parham encouraged his students to seek the gift of speaking in tongues (1901).

   b. Azusa Street Revival (1906); William Seymour founded Pentecostalism.

   c. World Missionary Conference was held to bring denominations together (1910).

2. Fundamentalism and Liberalism

   a. Harry Emerson Fosdick preached "Shall the Fundamentalists Win?" (1922)

   b. J. Gresham Machen defined liberalism as a different religion from Christianity (1923).

   c. "Neo-orthodox" theology was promoted through Karl Barth's commentary on Romans (1919).

   d. Dietrich Bonhoeffer urged German churches to resist Nazism.

3. The Ecumenical Movement

   a. World Council of Churches brought together neo-orthodox and liberals (1948).

   b. National Association of Evangelicals helped to distinguish evangelicals from fundamentalists (1942).

   c. Billy Graham launched large-scale evangelistic meetings (1949).

   d. Carl F. H. Henry wrote *The Uneasy Conscience of Modern Fundamentalism* (1947).

   e. Lausanne Covenant helped define evangelicalism (1974).

   f. Second Vatican Council removed the sentences of excommunication between Catholic Church and Eastern Orthodox (1962–1965).

   g. The Manhattan Declaration expressed common ground between churches on social issues (2009).

Key Terms

Azusa Street Revival (1906) — Often considered the beginning of modern Pentecostalism, this revival was led by African-American pastor William Seymour and located at the Apostolic Faith Mission on Azusa Street in Los Angeles. It emphasized the filling of the Holy Spirit, speaking in tongues, holiness, and faith healing.

Barmen Declaration (1934) — Statement that came from a meeting of German Protestant leaders in Barmen, Germany, held to oppose the so-called "German Christians" who were reinterpreting Christianity to conform to Nazi ideology. The Declaration's principal author was Karl Barth.

Ecumenical Movement — Movement that aimed to bring together Catholics, Protestants, Orthodox and other churches. The World Missionary Conference of 1910 and the World Council of Churches founded in 1948 were expressions of the ecumenical movement.

Evangelical (Neo-evangelical) — Expression of Christianity that seeks to establish and to maintain faithfulness to the biblical and confessional foundations of Christianity by emphasizing (1) the accuracy and authority of Scripture, (2) the exclusivity of salvation through personal faith in Jesus Christ, (3) the centrality of the sacrifice of Jesus Christ on the cross, (4) the need for global evangelism and cultural engagement, and (5) unity among like-minded Christians. In the nineteenth century and earlier, "evangelical" had been a synonym for "Protestant." In the twentieth century, the term "neo-evangelical" or "new evangelical" emerged to describe Christians who (unlike modernists) recognized Scripture as their authority and who (unlike fundamentalists) wanted to engage the culture instead of withdrawing from the culture. Eventually, "neo-evangelical" became simply "evangelical."

Fundamentalist — Twentieth-century fundamentalists resisted modernism by fighting verbally against any perceived threats to non-negotiable (or "fundamental") beliefs; many withdrew from meaningful engagement with the culture and lengthened their lists of non-negotiable beliefs to include for example, exclusive use of the King James Version and a pre-tribulational premillennial view of the end times. By the mid-twentieth century, "fundamentalists" typically referred to conservative Christians who focused on precise personal standards and on separation from every hint of liberalism.

Holiness Movement – Nineteenth-century movement that grew out of the Methodist church and focused on Christian sanctification. Holiness followers adhered to strict moral guidelines and abstained from worldly amusements. In the twentieth century some Holiness leaders, such as Charles Fox Parham, embraced speaking in tongues and faith healing.

Lausanne Covenant (1974) – Statement developed in Lausanne, Switzerland, at a convention—chaired by Billy Graham—of over 2,700 Christian leaders worldwide. This covenant became influential in defining evangelicalism.

Manhattan Declaration (2009) – Statement that recognized commonalities among evangelicals, conservative Protestants, Roman Catholics, and Orthodox on three specific moral issues: (1) profound, inherent, and equal dignity of every human being, (2) marriage as a conjugal union of man and woman, and (3) religious liberty.

Neo-orthodoxy – Theological movement, initiated by Swiss pastor Karl Barth, that reacted against theological liberalism by emphasizing God's sovereign self-revelation as the authority for Christian faith and practice. Unlike fundamentalists and evangelicals, Barth did not view Scripture as the inerrant written revelation of God. Instead, Scripture is a witness to Jesus, who is the one Word of God. Many neo-orthodox theologians eventually embraced patterns of thinking that were similar to theological modernism.

Pentecostalism – Expression of Christianity that emphasizes baptism by the Holy Spirit and speaking in tongues. Their name comes from the events described in Acts 2 when the Holy Spirit filled the disciples on the Day of Pentecost. Though distinct from the Holiness Movement, many early Pentecostals came from Holiness churches.

Second Vatican Council (1962) – Allowed translation of liturgies into native languages, recognized that non-Catholics "are not deprived of significance … in the mystery of salvation," and declared that "no one is to be forced [by ones' government] to act in a manner contrary to one's beliefs," but no key doctrine that separates Roman Catholics from Protestants, such as justification by faith or the extent of the pope's power, was changed.

Theological Liberalism (also, Theological Modernism) – Nineteenth-century movement that downplayed the authority of Scripture, focusing instead on imitation of Christ's ethics and on living with a deep awareness of a divine presence in all of life. Theological liberals altered Christian theology to fit the outlook of the modern world by separating Christian theology from traditional doctrines and biblical texts. In the twentieth century, theological liberalism developed into a movement that saw Christian principles as a foundation for accommodating the values of the culture. The twentieth-century American form of theological liberalism was known as theological modernism.

Before the Gathering

- In the *Christian History Made Easy* handbook read chapter 12.

- Preview the video segment Session 12 and PowerPoint® presentation chapter 12.

- Study Ephesians 4:1–16. Incorporate into your notes and discussion a few facts that you learned from this study.

- Complete the lesson in the Participant Guide for this session.

- If you will be using the video or PowerPoint® presentation, ensure that components are connected and tested beforehand.

- Locate the following three articles: "What Is an Evangelical?" (www.nae.net); "An Evangelical Manifesto" (www.anevangelicalmanifesto.com); and, "What Makes Evangelicalism Evangelical?" (www.albertmohler.com). Study each article carefully, developing a clear understanding of the term "evangelical." Choose one article that will be the most helpful for class members in this study. Print a copy of that article for each participant.

- Reflect on the past several weeks of study. Select a song that reflects important themes throughout this study. (Suggestions for songs can be found throughout pages 189–221 in the *Christian History Made Easy* handbook.) Plan to conclude this week's study by singing together.

- Pray for guidance as you lead this session.

Goals for the Gathering

Through this session, participants will be able to:

- Articulate how faithfulness to God's revelation of himself in Jesus Christ and in the Scriptures provides a necessary foundation for Christian unity and missions.

- Recognize distinctions between modernism, evangelicalism, and fundamentalism.

- Consider how particular patterns of life described in Ephesians 4 can contribute to the unity of the body of Christ and to the effectiveness of God's mission in the world.

Get Them Talking   (10 minutes)

Read Ephesians 4:1–16. Consider the following questions and statements for group discussion:

- Why should Christians be eager to seek unity and peace? (Eph. 4:3). [There is one body, one Spirit, one hope, one Lord Jesus, one faith, one baptism, one God and Father; relationships among Christians should reflect the oneness of God's work and of God himself.]

- What, according to Ephesians 4:8–11, is the practical impact of Jesus' enthronement with God the Father? [By defeating the powers of darkness and ascending to a place of exaltation over every earthly power, Jesus gained the capacity to provide gifts to his people, to bring them together in a new way with a new purpose.]

- What do shared theological beliefs have to do with church unity? (Eph. 4:13–14). [One aspect of Christian maturity includes not being "carried about by every wind of doctrine," distinguishing essential from nonessential beliefs and holding firmly to the essential beliefs.]

- What are the practical results of maturity and unity in Christ? (Eph. 4:15–16). [Answers will vary, but focus participants' attention on the growth of the body]

Take a Closer Look (30 to 60 minutes)

Watch the video segment Session 12. (30 minutes)

Optional: Review the content of the video using the PowerPoint® presentation chapter 12. (30 minutes)

Seek the Central Truth (15 minutes)

Distribute the article that you printed earlier. Discuss the meanings of modernism (or theological liberalism), evangelicalism, and fundamentalism. Consider the history of your own congregation in light of these terms.

- Is your church modernist, evangelical, or fundamentalist?
- Did it perhaps begin as a fundamentalist church and then become evangelical?
- Or has it perhaps drifted toward modernism in recent years?

Graciously consider together what direction your congregation could move in the future, then consider which direction your congregation should move.

Consider the following statement from the early twentieth century: "It is a startling and solemnizing fact that even as late as the twentieth century, the Great Command of Jesus Christ to carry the gospel to all mankind is still so largely unfulfilled.... The church is confronted today, as in no preceding generation, with a literally worldwide opportunity to make Christ known" (John R. Mott).

Discuss specific ways that your congregation can (1) become more unified, (2) articulate the gospel more clearly, and (3) participate more fully in God's global mission.

Wrap It Up (5 minutes)

End your time together by singing the song that you selected earlier.

Strongly encourage class members to complete the Participant Guide activities for this week.

Optional: Pray together as a group for persecuted Christians or, if time is short, ask participants to commit to praying at least once in the coming week for a specific region or country where our brothers and sisters face persecution.

Work Together

It would be a waste to learn so much and yet never to share it! Encourage each person to reflect on the past several weeks of study and then to select one individual or idea from church history that has been particularly meaningful to them. Help each person to make specific plans to share that story with one other person in the upcoming week. It might be with a child, a spouse, a student, a teacher, or a friend—but don't keep these stories to yourselves! Share them with others.

Session 13 (Optional)
Celebrating God's Work

Before the Gathering

Select one or more of the films to view with participants in your study. (See Historical Films list.) If you have a large group, you could choose two or three films and show different films in different rooms, allowing participants to choose as they arrive which film they wish to watch.

Review sections that relate to the selected film(s) in the *Christian History Made Easy* handbook, in this Leader Guide, and in the Participant Guide.

Plan for a variety of snacks to accompany the films.

Ensure that all video components are connected and tested beforehand.

Goals for the Gathering

Through this session, participants will:

- Enjoy fellowship together.

- Reinforce knowledge of particular events in church history by watching a film and reviewing that era together.

Get Them Talking   (10 minutes)

With all participants gathered together, review the main events of the era depicted in the film. Ask specific questions about that era of Christian history. Call attention to particular sections in the Participant Guide to help them remember these events.

Take a Closer Look   (times will vary)

Watch the selected film(s), providing snacks at intervals throughout the films.

Seek the Central Truth (15 minutes)

Gather all participants together. Discuss together how the film helped them to understand the story of Christianity. If participants have watched different films, summarize each film for everyone present.

Wrap It Up (5 minutes)

End with a reminder that Christianity is truly global. Pray together as a group for our persecuted brothers and sisters in Christ around the world.

Historical Films List

Not all of the films in the list below are suitable for every audience. Before showing any film, check with the leadership of your church or school to determine policies related to the use of films. Be certain that your organization has obtained any and all necessary permissions to show the selected film or that your use of the film falls within guidelines for educational fair use. None of the films in this list presents historical events perfectly or without selectivity; however, with the exception of *Inherit the Wind*, each film does present the events with a reasonable degree of accuracy. The value of *Inherit the Wind* is not in the accuracy of its portrayal of the Scopes trial but in what it tells us about how the modernist-fundamentalist debate was perceived in an increasingly secular society in the latter half of the twentieth century.

Ancient Christianity and the Middle Ages

The Agony and the Ecstasy (1965) (20th Century Fox, 2005) 138 min.

Apostle Paul and the Earliest Churches (Vision Video, 2004) 48 min.

Apostles' Creed (Abridged) (Vision Video, 2007) 120 min.

The Passion of Joan of Arc (1928) (Criterion, 1999) silent film, 82 min.

Perpetua: Early Church Martyr (Vision Video, 2009) 61 min.

Reformation, Expansion, and Enlightenment

Amazing Grace (20th Century Fox, 2007) Rated PG, 118 min.

Amistad (Dreamworks Video, 1999) Rated R, 155 min.

John Bunyan: Journey of a Pilgrim (Vision Video, 2007) 42 min.

KJB: Book That Changed the World (LionsGate, 2011) 94 min.

KJV: The Making of The King James Bible (Vision Video, 2010) 42 min.

Luther (MGM, 2004) Rated PG-13, 123 min.

A Man for All Seasons (1966) (Sony Pictures Home Entertainment, 2007) Rated G, 120 min.

The Mission (1986) (Warner Home Video, 2003) Rated PG, 125 min.

Uncommon Union: The Life and Love of Sarah and Jonathan Edwards (Vision Video, 2004) 54 min.

Wesley: A Heart Transformed (Vision Video, 2010) 117 min.

Modern and Contemporary Christianity

Bonhoeffer: Agent of Grace (Vision Video 2000) 90 min.

C. H. Spurgeon: the People's Preacher (Vision Video, 2010) 70 min.

C. S. Lewis: Beyond Narnia (Faith & Values Media, 2006) 54 min.

Gods and Generals (Turner Films, 2003) Rated PG-13, 219 min.

Heart of a Rebel (Lottie Moon Film, 2012) 90 min.

Inherit the Wind (1960) (United Artists, 2001) Rated PG, 128 min.

The Question of God: Sigmund Freud and C. S. Lewis (PBS, 2004) 225 min.

Shadowlands (HBO, 1994) Rated PG, 131 min.

The inclusion of a work does not mean endorsement of all its contents or other works by the same authors, artists, or studios.

Other DVD-Based Studies
For Individuals or Group Use

Christianity, Cults & Religions
Know what you believe and why!

Christians need to know what they believe. This excellent six-session DVD small group study teaches what the Bible says about God, Jesus, salvation, and more. It compares it to the teachings of other religions and cults. Covers Mormonism, Jehovah's Witnesses, Buddhism, Hinduism, Islam and more. Sessions led by Paul Carden, Director of The Centers for Apologetics Research and former co-host of "Bible Answer Man" radio program.

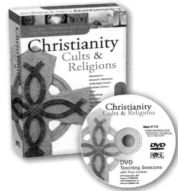

771X Complete Kit 9781596364134
771DV Leader Pack 9781596364271
784X Leaders Guide...9781596364288
785X Participants Guide......................................9781596364295
404X Christianity, Cults & Religions pamphlet..................9789901981403

Four Views of the End Times
Cut through the confusion about the *Book of Revelation*

What does the Bible actually say about the end times that lead to the return of Jesus Christ? The differing ideas that divide believers into four major points-of-view are examined in this Four Views of the End Times DVD-based small group study. This new six-session study shows four different Revelation time lines and tackles Dispensational Premillennialism, Postmillennialism, Historic Premillennialism, and Amillennialism. For each view, the objective study includes simple definitions, explanation and discussion of supporting Scriptures, an overview of the view's popularity, and a focus on what we can gain from studying this perspective, and common questions and answers.

770X Complete Kit 9781596364127
770DV Leader Pack 9781596364240
782X Leader Guide: Four Views...............................9781596364257
783X Participants Guide: Four Views..........................9781596364264
350X Four Views of the End Times pamphlet...................9781596360891

Feasts of the Bible
Connect the Hebrew roots of Christianity and the symbolism within each feast

Some Christians miss the importance of the biblical feasts, seeing them as merely "Jewish" holidays, but Scripture says these are the Feasts of the Lord God, established for all people for all time. Now you can connect the Hebrew roots of Christianity and the symbolism within each feast that points to Jesus Christ. The Feasts and Holidays of the Bible will also show you how to conduct your own Christian Passover Seder, where you will learn how all the Old Testament Passover activities point symbolically to Jesus.

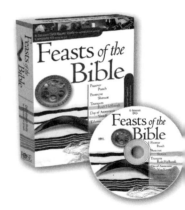

101X Complete Kit 9781596364646
101DV Leader Pack 9781596364653
102X Leaders Guide...9781596364660
103X Participants Guide......................................9781596364677
455X Feasts of the Bible pamphlet...........................9781890947583
108X Messiah in the Feasts of Israel book....................9780970261977